The Power of Experiments

The Power of Experiments

Decision Making in a Data-Driven World

Michael Luca and Max H. Bazerman

The MIT Press

Cambridge, Massachusetts | London, England

First MIT Press paperback edition, 2021
© 2020 Michael Luca and Max H. Bazerman

This book was set in ITC Stone Serif Std and ITC Stone Sans Std by Toppan Best-set Premedia Limited. Printed and bound in the United States of America.

Library of Congress Cataloging-in-Publication Data

Names: Luca, Michael, author. | Bazerman, Max H., author.
Title: The power of experiments : decision making in a data-driven world / Michael Luca, Max H. Bazerman.
Description: Cambridge, Massachusetts : The MIT Press, [2020] | Includes bibliographical references and index.
Identifiers: LCCN 2019029932 | ISBN 9780262043878 (hardcover) | ISBN 9780262542272 (paperback) | ISBN 9780262358255 (ebook)
Subjects: LCSH: Economics--Psychological aspects. | Experimental economics. | Decision making. | Psychology.
Classification: LCC HB74.P8 L83 2020 | DDC 330.01/9--dc23
LC record available at https://lccn.loc.gov/2019029932

10 9 8 7 6 5 4 3 2

Contents

Preface   vii
Acknowledgments   xi

Part I: Breaking Out of the Lab   1

1:   **The Power of Experiments   3**
2:   **The Rise of Experiments in Psychology and Economics   17**
3:   **The Rise of Behavioral Experiments in Policymaking   45**

Part II: Experiments in the Tech Sector   59

4:   **From the Behavioral Insights Team to Booking.com   61**
5:   **#AirbnbWhileBlack   75**
6:   **eBay's $50 Million Advertising Mistake   91**
7:   **Deep Discounts at Alibaba   99**
8:   **Shrouded Fees at StubHub   105**
9:   **Market-Level Experiments at Uber   113**
10: **The Facebook Blues   121**

Part III: Experimenting for the Social Good   133

11: **Behavioral Experiments for the Social Good   135**
12: **Healthy, Wealthy, and Wise   145**

13: The Behavior Change for Good Project 161

14: The Ethics of Experimentation 173

15: A Final Case for Experiments and Some Concluding Lessons 177

Notes 189

Index 203

Preface

How many experiments do you think you've participated in over the past year? We're talking about randomized controlled trials—experiments designed to test the impact of different treatments by randomly assigning you and other participants (often called subjects) to various treatment conditions, like those you might have participated in if you took Psych 101 or if you've tried out an experimental drug.

So, what's your number? At first blush, you might think the answer is zero. But unless you live in a bunker with no Internet access, you've likely participated in *many* experiments over the past year. If you logged onto Facebook right now, there's a good chance you'd be an unwitting subject in a variety of the company's ongoing experiments as you scroll through your News Feed and peruse the ads being shown to you. You are also likely to be a test subject if you search for an item on Google, watch a movie on Netflix, respond to email surveys, or call companies for customer support.

In a dramatic departure from its historic role as an esoteric tool for academic research, the randomized controlled trial has gone mainstream. Historically, experimental methods may have been alien to the managerial toolkit. These days, companies like Google wouldn't dare make a major change in their platforms without first looking at experiments to understand how it would influence user behavior. From startups to international conglomerates to government agencies, organizations have a new tool to develop frameworks and test ideas, and to understand the impact of the products and services they are providing.

We are in the early days of the age of experiments. Experiments help to complement intuition and guesswork with evidence-based decision making. We've seen many experiments lead to large returns for organizations—as when a simple experiment allowed eBay to learn that it was wasting millions of dollars per year in an advertising campaign. The discoveries that experiments generate are largely a good thing: good for governments, which can use experimental results to better design and deliver services; good for companies, which can use experimental results to improve their human resources practices and offer better products; and, when carefully designed and monitored, good for employees, customers, and citizens as well. We'll highlight success stories arising from experiments and the lessons we can draw from them.

At the same time, we've seen plenty of experiments that were poorly executed or interpreted, yielding misleading conclusions or wasted time and effort. Even in the best of worlds, experiments can be challenging to design and interpret—and require managerial judgment. For example, when gym chain 24 Hour Fitness ran experiments aimed at identifying ways to increase attendance rates, they found that many of the interventions that increased gymgoing in the short run were often considerably less impactful when the results were tracked over several months.

Designing and interpreting experiments can be challenging tasks, requiring a unique combination of skills. In the age of experiments, effective managers increasingly need frameworks for going from experimental results to decisions. This book will help to develop and draw out principles that will help managers make the most of experimental results.

Experiments can also raise concerns for customers and policymakers—especially as the world's stock of experiments and results is mostly sitting in corporate databases, hidden from the public and being used for unknown purposes. Experiments can feel complex, invasive, and Big Brotherish, especially when we realize we've been totally oblivious to our regular participation in them. Some corporate experiments may risk being good for companies but bad for their customers. As we'll see, StubHub ran an experiment that led it to conclude that it should tack on ticket fees at the last minute, just before a purchase, rather than making them transparent. The value of the experiment to customers is dubious, even as its value to the company is clear.

In the end, an experiment is a tool, one that can make us better or worse off, depending on who is running it, what their goals are, and what they mean when they say the experiment "worked." Excited by the promise of experimental methods, while cognizant of their perils, we wrote this book to shed light on the evolving role of experiments, including the insights they have yielded and their effect on the public discourse. Our goal is to help readers gain an appreciation of the value of experiments and avoid common pitfalls. We'll demystify the experimental method, which is at times cast in alarmist tones.

We will begin (part I) with a broad discussion of the potential of experiments and the factors that have led to their proliferation. In the process, we'll describe the nerdy and fascinating history of the experimental revolution, including the earliest known experiments, advances in scientific methods, the rise of social science labs and field experiments, and the recent proliferation of companies and governments running their own experiments. Next (part II), we will cover the central role experiments play in the tech sector—drawing out lessons and best practices from a series of notable experiments covering companies ranging from Airbnb to Uber to eBay. Moving beyond the tech sector, we'll examine (part III) how behavioral experiments in organizations are helping to shed light on health, education, and financial decision making—leading to processes and products that better account for the many quirks of human behavior.

Over the course of the book, you'll get a closer look at the types of experiments companies and governments are running—and the decisions they are informing. And throughout, we'll draw out the insights that can be gained from experiments and where and when they are most useful. Our goal is to shed light on the role that experiments are playing in the world around us. By the end, we hope you'll walk away with an appreciation of the power of experiments.

Acknowledgments

We first met when Mike was a new faculty member at the Harvard Business School and Max was returning from a sabbatical at Berkeley. We quickly realized we liked chatting with each other—about everything from food (we're both fans of pizza and Indian food) to dogs to the merits of Palo Alto vs. Berkeley to experiments, and how they were changing the landscape of research and practice. After a while we decided to create a project-based class together, Behavioral Insights, which took hundreds of Harvard graduate students to some combination of London, Paris, and the Netherlands to work with government agencies to develop experiments to help their agencies work better. Increasingly excited about the role experiments were playing in practice, we led a faculty excursion of more than 20 of our Harvard Business School faculty colleagues to the Bay Area to learn about the new world of experimentation in the tech sector. We developed some course materials around behavioral insights. Eventually we decided to write this book.

During this time, we had each been thinking about experiments more broadly. We were doing research in the area. We also wrote a few broader articles on experimentation, in addition to some case studies we developed and taught in the MBA program. This book builds on and develops these ideas; some passages are excerpted or adapted from articles and case studies we have written.[1] We are also continuing work on this agenda, and are drawing on sections of this book as we develop new case studies on initiatives such as the Behavior Change for Good project.

Our work has been influenced by our interactions over the last few years with colleagues, mentors, and friends, including Susan Athey, Mike Bailey, Netta Barak-Corren, Amy Bernstein, Iris Bohnet, Lis Costa, Geoff Donaker, Angela Duckworth, Ray Fisman, Frances Frei, Duncan Gilchrist, Francesca Gino, Ed Glaeser, Avi Goldfarb, Josh Greene, Shane Greenstein, David Halpern, Karen Huang, Ginger Jin, Danny Kahneman, Ariella Kristal, Katy Milkman, Sarah Moshary, Jonah Rockoff, Todd Rogers, Al Roth, Ovul Sezer, Jon Smith, Scott Stern, Steve Tadelis, Chia Tsay, Ashley Whillans, and Ting Zhang. The book also builds on work with our academic collaborators, including Daisy Dai, Ben Edelman, Jeff Fossett, Oliver Hauser, Hyunjin Kim, Deepak Malhotra, Patrick Rooney, Michael Sanders, and Dan Svirsky—as well as research assistance and collaborations on teaching materials, including with Stephanie Chan, Evan DeFilippis, Tiffany Fan, Marie Lawrence, Patrick Rooney, and Jenina Soto.

We are thankful to our colleagues in the Negotiation, Organizations, and Markets unit at HBS: John Beshears, Alison Wood Brooks, Katie Coffman, Christine Exley, Francesca Gino, Jerry Green, Brian Hall, Deepak Malhotra, Kathleen McGinn, Kevin Mohan, Matthew Rabin, Josh Schwartzstein, Jim Sebenius, Andrei Shleifer, Mario Small, Guhan Subramanian, Andy Wasynczuk, Ashley Whillans, and Julian Zlatev. We are lucky to be surrounded by kind and caring colleagues who are always ready to chat about, well, anything and everything, ranging from the book to whether it's more efficient to take the stairs or elevator to which bakery has the best cakes in Boston (in case you're wondering: Flour Bakery and Party

Favors). Over the years, we've had many fruitful (and cake-ful) conversations with our colleagues that have shaped our perspectives on experiments.

Members of the broader HBS community have been supportive throughout our writing process. While writing this book, Mike designed a new MBA course on the role of experiments in managerial decisions—based in part on an encouraging discussion with Dean Nitin Nohria, who has been supportive of the project from the start. Frances Frei, Francesca Gino, Shane Greenstein, Deepak Malhotra, V. G. Narayanan, Mike Norton, and Jan Rivkin provided valuable feedback and guidance related to the course. Tiffany Fan and Jeff Fossett were amazing teaching assistants for the course, and their work and input helped to shape our views. Our class discussion helped to develop and refine the ideas in this book, just as the students in our Behavioral Insights course have. It's been fun and rewarding to watch them become part of the behavioral insights and experimental movements.

Adam Colman, Hengchen Dai, Andy O'Connell, Todd Rogers, Al Roth, and Steve Tadelis provided insightful feedback on parts of the manuscript. The book is far better as a result. We also benefited from the amazing editing of Katie Shonk, Max's long-time research assistant, coauthor, and editor. Elizabeth Sweeny proofread, error-checked, and generally fixed what needed to be fixed. Our insightful and supportive editor at MIT Press, Emily Taber, provided thought-provoking feedback and valuable guidance throughout.

Dedication

From Mike: This book is dedicated to my family—my kids, Teddy and Toby; my wife, Dara; and my mom, Ann.

From Max: This book is dedicated to my conceptual family of experimentalists, who have educated me over the last decade on how to have impact through experimentation. This list includes Mahzarin Banaji, Netta Barak-Corren, John Beshears, Iris Bohnet, Eugene Caruso, Dolly Chugh, Lucas Coffman, Nick Epley, Francesca Gino, Josh Greene, Karen Huang, Danny Kahneman, Ariella Kristal, Deepak Malhotra, Kathleen McGinn, Katy Milkman, Don Moore, Keith Murnighan, Todd Rogers, Ovul Sezer, Lisa Shu, Ann Tenbrunsel, Chia-Jung Tsay, Ashley Whillans, and Ting Zhang.

Part I   Breaking Out of the Lab

1
The Power of Experiments

The UK tax authority, Her Majesty's Revenue and Customs (HMRC), works hard to make sure that people pay their taxes on time. Nonetheless, tens of billions of pounds of taxes go unpaid each year. When someone fails to pay her taxes, the government sends a reminder letter. In principle, the government has other options, such as taking her to court or garnishing her wages. But this would be costly and inconvenient for everyone, so the hope is that the taxpayer will simply respond to the letter by paying her back taxes.

While the original letter sent by HMRC to delinquent taxpayers is not publicly available, it historically read something like this:[1]

Dear Sarah,

We are writing to inform you that we have still not received your tax payment of £___. It is imperative that you contact us.

[Contact information here]
HMRC

While the identity of the original letter writer is now shrouded in the mists of time, their work—much like Frankenstein's monster—

lived on. HMRC cranked out the same letter year after year and sent it to every delinquent taxpayer in the UK; but many people continued to ignore the government's pleas. Life went on. And, like so many other defective systems found in companies and governments, no one knew why the inferior system persisted—or even recognized that it was inferior. But it's easy to see why recipients may have taken the letter for granted. To a tax department employee facing a long list of tasks, sending a reminder letter to delinquent taxpayers must have felt about as fun as a visit to the dentist.

In 2010, deep within the UK government, an obscure team of eight social scientists and civil servants assembled to form the Behavioural Insights Team (BIT)—the brainchild of a novel academic-turned-policymaker named David Halpern and a whip-smart ambitious civil servant named Owain Service. Their mission? To improve policy and government through the use of behavioral science. The team had lots of ideas, though no formal authority or partners. But where HMRC saw administrative hassle, BIT saw opportunity. In fact, the team saw no better starting point than taking the dullest of all letters and sprucing it up with a little behavioral science to help motivate people to pay up. You might be wondering, how much could the wording of the letter matter? The genius of Halpern's idea wasn't the decision to rewrite the letter, but rather the recognition that they didn't need to wonder whether the wording matters—they could just find out.

Halpern worked hard to persuade Her Majesty's tax collectors to allow them not only to rewrite the letter, but also to conduct an experiment to measure the effect of the rewriting.[2] The trial was years in the making. In 2007 (before BIT was founded, but after Halpern had the initial idea), he brought an excellent social psychologist—Robert Cialdini—to 10 Downing Street to discuss his work and opportunities to bring behavioral insights into policy. In parallel, HMRC began to work with Cialdini to rewrite their letter.

Halpern walked HMRC through the details of experimentation and explained why it would be valuable to run an experiment to test the rewritten letter. As part of his persuading, he offered to help HMRC find a full-time employee to work on experimental trials, which would allow the tax department to retain operational control of the experiment and ensure that the data collected would not leave HMRC's hands. That person was Michael Hallsworth, a civil servant who would eventually go on to earn a PhD in economics and publish some of the tax trial results.

In the first set of trials, the experimenters picked a set of taxpayers to send letters to. They sent the original letter to one randomly selected group and a slightly altered version to another. The new letter added a single sentence to the original letter that you read above: "By now, 9 out of 10 people in your town have paid their taxes." The results of this addition were striking: The percentage of people paying their taxes increased from 35.8% to 37.8%. That might not sound like much, but it amounts to millions of pounds when scaled to everyone who owes back taxes.

Hallsworth and BIT went on to test many variants of the tax letter. In one set of experiments, they tested these five one-liners, which could easily double as the world's most boring small talk for a first date:

Basic norm	Nine out of ten people pay their tax on time.
Country norm	Nine out of ten people in the UK pay their tax on time.
Minority norm	Nine out of ten people in the UK pay their tax on time. You are currently in the very small minority of people who have not paid us yet.
Gain-framed public good	Paying tax means we all gain from vital public services like the NHS, roads, and schools.
Loss-framed public good	Not paying tax means we all lose out on vital public services like the NHS, roads, and schools.

Each of these messages was sent to about 17,000 people in England, Wales, and Northern Ireland. Before we tell you what happened, grab a pen. Write down which of these lines you think did best.

In this group of messages, the "minority norm" was most effective, although all of the messages were more effective than the baseline letter. HMRC collected 1.9 million pounds of tax revenue from sending the minority norm letter, which would have amounted to 11.3 million pounds if all the letters from the experiment were sent out using this messaging. Thanks to this letter, more money was collected, and money was collected earlier than it would have been otherwise. Further experiments found that the statements "Most people in your local area pay on time" or "Most people with a debt like yours have paid it by now" made the letter even more effective, as did addressing the taxpayer by their first name, such as "Dear John."

Hallsworth spent his days at HMRC writing and testing different letters.[3] He tested short letters and long letters (short ones were more effective), nice letters and mean letters (mean letters can work well, but they can trigger public outcry). The tests went on and on. We haven't asked him, but we like to imagine that Hallsworth has ported these insights into other areas of his life as well—and that he now sends short behaviorally informed love letters to his wife, such as "I love you more than 90% of husbands love their wives ..."

It became clear that HMRC's original letter had left tens of millions of pounds per year on the table—money that is slowly being brought back, thanks to tiny tweaks to a long-ignored letter. After these initial experiments, the agency became excited about adopting experimental methods and paying doting attention to the details. HMRC now has its own behavioral team, which continues to run trials. The agency has learned a great deal about what works, what doesn't, and what backfires. And continued experimentation allows HMRC to ensure it isn't leaving money on the table due to a badly designed letter.

BIT, meanwhile, quickly became the talk of the policy town. The team moved on to other policy areas, using behavioral experiments to help solve some of the nation's most stubborn problems. Within five years, BIT was running experiments in schools to reduce dropout rates, in employment centers to help people find jobs, and in hospitals to get more patients to show up for appointments. By 2018, BIT had run more than 500 randomized controlled trials, and its approach has diffused throughout the world. We both sit on the team's academic advisory board and are excited about the progress made both by the UK Behavioural Insights Team and the broader use of experiments around the globe.

After this high-profile case study, the use of behavioral insights to help improve government operations caught on in earnest, inspiring the creation of similar teams around the globe. There are now dozens of teams like BIT running experiments within governments to test ideas in close to real time, as we'll continue to explore in the book.

The BIT tax letter experiment demonstrates the value of an experimental mindset, even for organizations that are new to experiments and even for experiments of the simplest variety (swap out a line of a letter that is already being sent). Yet we're early in the age of experiments: despite the model provided by this experiment's success and simplicity, most governmental tax departments still do not run experiments to test their approaches to tax collection.

Perhaps most importantly for BIT, the experiment demonstrated the group's value to skeptical stakeholders. It's perhaps unsurprising that many of the new behavioral insights teams cropping up in other countries have run tax experiments to show off what they are capable of. This points to an important role that experiments can play: demonstrating the value of a new product or service. Nonprofits and startups increasingly are having their core products evaluated via experiments so that they can show their value to stakeholders (or change course if it turns out they aren't creating value!).

A Quick Aside: The Anatomy of an Experiment

Throughout the book, we'll walk through a variety of stories that illustrate why organizations run experiments and how they can make the most of them. We won't get into technical detail about experimental statistics, as there are textbooks that already do that. But before proceeding, here are a few informal definitions surrounding experiments that will pop up throughout the book, illustrated with the tax letter example:

Concept	What is it?	In the BIT example
Control group	This group serves as a basis of comparison for the treatment group.	The group that received the baseline tax letter with no text added to it.
Treatment group(s)	Experimental participants in these groups will get an additional treatment (relative to what the control group receives). A randomized control trial may have one or more treatment groups.	The groups that received the tax letter with various sentences about social norms added.
Independent variable	The variable whose effect you are trying to measure.	The varied content of the tax letter being sent (e.g., a variable indicating whether a social norm message was included).
Dependent variable	The outcome(s) of interest.	Whether the recipient paid her taxes on time. Alternative dependent variables might include the amount paid or whether the taxpayer complained about the letter.

Concept	What is it?	In the BIT example
Average treatment effect	The effect of the treatment on the general population of individuals being treated, on average. Under certain conditions in an experiment, this can be derived by comparing the average outcomes of the treatment vs. control group.	For the population sampled in the tax letter experiment, the treatment effect = payment rates (treatment group) – payment rates (control group) = 35.1 – 33.6 = 1.5%. On average, the additional text increased repayment rates during the time period being analyzed by 1.5%.

The Book of Daniel

The Behavioural Insights Team played a key role in bringing an experimental mindset into government, but they did not invent the idea. The person often identified as the earliest experimentalist is Daniel—yes, that Daniel, from the Bible.

The book of Daniel, believed to have been written between 167 and 164 BC, tells the story of how King Nebuchadnezzar of Babylonia attacked Jerusalem and captured Israelite prisoners, whom he took with him back to Babylon. The king assigned his chief official, Ashpenaz, to select the most handsome, intelligent, and healthy prisoners to be trained to serve in the royal court. For three years, the king ordered, the prisoners were to be taught the Babylonian language and fed the same wine and food as court members. But Daniel, one of the prisoners, vowed to himself that he would not be made "ritually unclean" by the court's food and drink.[4] He asked the guard who was watching him and three of his friends to feed them only vegetables and water for 10 days. "Then compare us with the young men who are eating the food of the royal court, and base your decision [about whom to add to the court] on how we look," he asked.[5] The guard agreed, and the improvised experiment began.

After 10 days, the guard judged that Daniel and his friends appeared significantly healthier and stronger than the men who had subsisted on the royal diet. Consequently, they were able to continue their healthy lifestyle for the duration of the three-year training period. The men also reportedly benefited from divine intervention during this time: "God gave the four young men knowledge and skill in literature and philosophy," the Bible says. "In addition, he gave Daniel skill in interpreting visions and dreams."[6] After the three years were up, the four men impressed the king with their knowledge, which surpassed that of "any fortune-teller or magician."[7] The king ultimately chose Daniel and his fellow vegetarians over the omnivores for his court—a victory that may not surprise modern-day vegetarians.

Daniel appears to have sketched out the rough outlines of what we would now call a clinical trial: he chose himself and his friends as consenting human subjects, the Babylonian court members as his control group, and a vegetarian diet as the therapeutic agent being tested. But, not surprisingly, Daniel's experiment falls far short of today's standards for clinical trials. Modern experiments compare the outcomes of one group with those of a comparable group receiving a control treatment; people in both groups are enrolled, treated, and followed over the same time period. The groups may be created through random assignment or some other assignment method. In contrast, the two diets that Daniel studied may not have been mutually exclusive (the Babylonians' diet may have included vegetables and water); the trial was not randomized (those in the intervention group selected themselves and the treatment); the sample size of the intervention group was tiny (four people); and the size of the control group is unknown.[8] Finally, a single observer, the guard, measured the results based on subjects' appearance rather than with more objective methods.

Fifteen Centuries Later

After Daniel's study, 1,500 years passed before another known case of clinical experimentation was documented. In the sixteenth century, Ambroise Paré served four French kings as a member of the somewhat hair-raising profession of "barber surgeon"—a medieval medic whose duties included cutting off both hair and limbs, as needed, often on the battlefield. One day, while attending soldiers during battle, Paré writes, he ran out of the boiling oil that was routinely used to cauterize wounds and replaced it with what he, apparently, had lying around at the time: a "digestive made of oil of yolks of eggs, oil of roses, and turpentine."[9] Paré tossed and turned that night, fretting that he would find those whose wounds he had not cauterized dead from what he now feared was "poison." Rising early the next morning, Paré found, to his surprise, that the soldiers he had treated with his homemade tincture felt "but little pain," while those treated with boiling oil were "feverish with much pain and swelling about their wounds." And while the experimental design was again far from perfect, the results of Paré's accidental experiment paved the way toward a more effective (and evidently less painful) means of treating infection than cauterization.

Two hundred years later, James Lind, a surgeon, carried out what some consider to be the first controlled clinical trial of the modern era.[10] In 1747, while working as a surgeon on a British navy ship, Lind planned a comparative trial to identify the best treatment for scurvy, which was running rampant among the crew. He selected 12 sailors "in the scurvy" whose cases were "as similar as I could have them": they all had "putrid gums, the spots and lassitude, with weakness of the knees."[11] Moreover, the victims were all on the same diet, which included the rather eclectic menu of water gruel sweetened with sugar for breakfast, fresh mutton broth for lunch, "barley and raisins, rice and currants, sago and wine" for dinner, not to mention light puddings and boiled biscuit between meals. Lind divided the 12 patients into pairs and assigned a different treatment to each pair: one pair was ordered to drink one quart of cider each per day; another took two spoonfuls of vinegar three times a day; one unlucky pair was given seawater; members of another pair were given two oranges and one lemon to eat daily; and so on. Lind observed the patients and found that, after about a week, the two supplementing with citrus recovered better than the others. Proving that evidence is only one piece of the puzzle of enacting beneficial change, it took another 50 years before the British navy made lemon juice a compulsory ingredient in sailors' diets.

In 1882, Louis Pasteur tested the effectiveness of vaccines while simultaneously launching the concept of controlled trials to the wider world. Pasteur, of course, pioneered the theory that a weak form of a disease could lend immunity to a more virulent form of the disease. The well-known veterinarian Hippolyte Rossignol, who might be considered the first anti-vaxxer, publicly challenged Pasteur's early findings on vaccines. The two eminent scientists faced off in a widely publicized part-contest, part-experiment held at a farm just south of Paris.

With reporters from across France and as far away as London looking on, Pasteur vaccinated an experimental group of 25 sheep against anthrax and designated another 25 sheep as the control group. All 50 animals were then given a lethal dose of anthrax. The contestants agreed that for Pasteur to be declared the winner, every control sheep would have to die, and every vaccinated sheep would have to survive—a very high standard as compared to current statistical methods.[12] Within two days, Pasteur proved the undisputed winner: all of the vaccinated sheep remained healthy, the 25 control sheep were dead, and the concept of the control group was born (though, clearly, the concept of treating animal test participants humanely was still a long way off).

Looking at agricultural field experiments in the 1920s, the British statistician Ronald Fisher invented a statistical test to figure out whether a manipulation in an experiment had a statistically meaningful effect. Fisher also highlighted the importance of randomly assigning study participants to different experimental groups. Fisher laid out other experimental protocols that remain common to this day, including replication (repeating experiments and measurements to reduce uncertainty about sources of variance) and blocking (arranging experimental units into similar groups to reduce irrelevant sources of variation).[13]

In 1946, the United Kingdom's Medical Research Council (MRC) conducted the first randomized control clinical trial in a study of the ability of a new antibiotic, streptomycin, to treat patients with very advanced pulmonary tuberculosis. Supplies of streptomycin were limited, and the MRC wanted to determine whether the drug would be more beneficial to severely afflicted TB patients than bed rest alone. Subjects' enrollment in the treatment or control group was based on random sampling, and the investigators, as well as those who interpreted patients' X-ray scans monthly, were blind to their treatment assignment. Moreover, because only a limited supply of streptomycin was available, the scientists were able to withhold a potentially successful treatment from the patients in the control group without raising ethical concerns. The results showed that streptomycin was indeed beneficial to very ill TB patients. Streptomycin is still used to treat TB and other serious infections, and the study's randomization became standard experimental procedure.

In recent decades, the medical community has been an early adopter of experimental methods. However, progress has been uneven and is still rapidly evolving. Take hormone replacement therapy. In 1966, Brooklyn-based gynecologist Robert Wilson published his book *Feminine Forever* on the use of estrogen as a long-term remedy for women's aging issues. Previously, women took estrogen only for short-term relief from hot flashes, sweating, and other uncomfortable symptoms of menopause. Wilson argued that menopause was an illness that could be treated by taking estrogen to replace the hormones that naturally diminished in women's ovaries as they aged. With this argument, hormone replacement therapy (HRT)—taking prescription estrogen as a preventative measure—was born.

By the mid-1990s, the American Heart Association, the American College of Physicians, and the American College of Obstetrics and Gynecologists were recommending HRT as a long-term treatment for conditions related to women's aging, such as heart disease and osteoporosis, based on the results of several cohort studies, particularly the large-scale Nurses' Health Study. For the next twenty years, many doctors went from prescribing hormone therapy only as a treatment for postmenopausal women with severe symptoms to using it as a preventative measure for a broader set of women with symptoms.

The problem is, this was the wrong interpretation of the data. As it turned out, the analysis suffered from an issue that frequently occurs in observational data—selection bias. Selection bias occurs when the people who receive an intervention (e.g., a product or service) of interest are systematically different from those who don't. In this situation, a comparison of those who do and don't receive a treatment conflates the impact of treatment itself and underlying differences in the populations arising from nonrandom assignment to the treatment. This can make it challenging to draw causal conclusions from correlational data. In this context, the women who were getting hormone therapy were disproportionately of higher socioeconomic status, and tended to have better access to medical care—which were likely affecting their health decisions and outcomes in myriad ways. For example, women who received hormone therapy in the observational analyses were also less likely to die in car accidents, even after controlling for observable differences across groups.

An experiment using random assignment of hormone therapy was in order. Harvard Medical School physician and researcher JoAnn Manson was among the lead investigators to experimentally test the impact of hormone therapy. She and her colleagues in the Women's Health Initiative (WHI) found results that contrasted with the observational data in some respects. In fact, instead of reducing the odds of heart disease, the experiment showed that hormone therapy was actually *increasing* the odds of heart disease. The results sent shockwaves through the medical community. Many doctors went from heavily prescribing hormone therapy to not prescribing it at all. This made it difficult for some women to receive hormone therapy even if they had severe symptoms.

The experiment points to the importance of random assignment in experiments, as well as the fact that interpreting experimental data requires judgment and a deep understanding of an issue. New work by Dr. Manson and others suggests that the medical community may have overreacted to the new experimental results as well, as the magnitude of the risks of heart disease from HRT is relatively low, especially for women in their 50s who were the most likely to need HRT to address postmenopausal symptoms. Moreover, hormone therapy had some other benefits, such as lower risk of fracture and diabetes. Over time, clinical guidance has evolved—with the medical community gaining a deeper appreciation of the potential for selection bias, the value of an experiment, the complexity of a treatment's effects, and the judgment required in making decisions even from experimental data.

Today, medical research is a significant enterprise in society. In 2010, the United States National Institutes of Health spent $10.7 billion on medical research, $7.4 billion on genetics-related research, $6 billion on disease prevention research, $5.8 billion on cancer research, and $5.7 billion on biotechnology.[14] In 2012, $119 billion was spent in the United States on medical research, accounting for 45% of the world's biomedical research spending. And experiments have become an important part of this research.

Human longevity has risen steadily thanks to evidence-based medical advances, including the development of vaccines to treat and prevent the spread of diseases such as measles and polio; new, more effective treatments for cancer; the discovery of effective antibiotics to cure a variety of diseases; and the development of statins to treat cardiovascular disease—to name just a few of the more significant breakthroughs achieved through clinical research. Experiments have been key to the development of this knowledge.

The experimental revolution now reaches far beyond medicine. Long before the UK tax collectors were experimenting on taxpayers, psychologists were experimenting in the lab. Economists and other social scientists began experimenting in the lab as well, and extended their experimentation to real-world contexts, from policy to business. Experiments are increasingly entering the mainstream among governments, tech companies, and old-economy firms. Many large corporations have used experiments, and tech giants such as Google, Facebook, and Uber run thousands of experiments each year.

But, as we have noted, these are still the early days of experiments in organizations. Far too often, organizations continue to rely on intuition rather than evidence to make decisions. We like to have faith in our intuition, but the fact is, it's often flat-out wrong. To take a simple example, during sabbatical, one of us (Mike) was in the habit for a while of going to a particular Starbucks drive-through for his morning coffee, which often meant sitting in a line of cars. After a month or so, he decided to test his intuition that the drive-through was faster than parking and going inside to wait in line, so he parked his old Hyundai Elantra in one of the many open spaces (in retrospect, the open spaces should have been a clue that his intuition was flawed) and marched into the store, which was ... empty! His faulty intuition was easily replaced by data. Formal experiments similarly replace intuition with data, but on a much larger scale and with more exacting methods.

2
The Rise of Experiments in Psychology and Economics

As we've seen, many of the earliest experimentalists focused on medical research. But in the past century or more, experimentation has expanded well beyond medicine and the hard sciences and into the social sciences, business, and policy. Another early adopter of experimental methods, the field of psychology, has played an important role in catalyzing the rise of behavioral experiments, such as BIT's tax letter experiment. In this chapter, we'll walk through some of the history of experimental methods (and experimental laboratories) in psychology. We'll then turn to the central role that psychology played in creating the field of behavioral economics, and ultimately in creating the behavioral policy units that are now running experiments in governments at an impressive scale around the globe.

A Brief History of Experimental Psychology

Experimental psychology as we know it sprang from the "mental philosophy" of the British philosopher John Locke, who postulated in his landmark 1690 book *An Essay Concerning Human*

Understanding that the human mind is a *tabula rasa*, or blank slate. The notion that we acquire knowledge through experience, rather than possessing innate understanding, was a radical one at the time. Locke sparked the longstanding "nature versus nurture" debate in psychology. But before the first true experimental psychologists built on Locke's understanding of the brain, a procession of pseudo-scientists traipsed through history: hypnotists, phrenologists, and spiritualists, many of whom traveled from town to town peddling their unorthodox methods from a telltale bag of tricks. The admonition "You need to have your head examined" originated not as a rebuke but as a well-meaning suggestion to seek out the services of one of the traveling phrenologists of the 1800s.[1]

German doctor Wilhelm Wundt opened the first psychology laboratory at the University of Leipzig in 1879.[2] Wundt guided more than 180 students to doctoral degrees at his lab and wrote prolifically. In the 1870s, G. Stanley Hall, a philosophy professor at Antioch College in Ohio, became enamored of Wundt's experimental psychology. He earned a doctorate at Harvard, where he met William James (brother of the great novelist Henry James), a pioneer in the new field of psychology, who believed that laboratory research was incapable of capturing the complexity of the human mind. By 1883, Hall realized his dream of conducting research, founding the first psychology lab in America at Johns Hopkins University.

In the 1890s, psychology labs popped up across the United States, aiming to bring the experimental methods of the hard sciences to the study of the human mind. A notable researcher of this era was Edward Bradford Titchener, who sought to determine the structure of consciousness through carefully devised experiments involving an "introspector" and an "observer." For 30 years, college instructors used Titchener's four-volume *Experimental Psychology: A Manual of Laboratory Practice* (1901–1905) to teach both themselves and their students basic laboratory methods and classic experiments.

The most famous psychologist of the first half of the twentieth century, Sigmund Freud, was distinctly not part of the evolution of experimental psychology. Freud based his theories on anecdotal observation, making them difficult to validate in the lab; those that were tested often failed to hold water. Freud's disconnect from the emerging focus on experimental methods made him a controversial scientific figure. But his big ideas inspired entire fields of psychological research that followed, including his notion that unconscious processes shape our judgments and behavior, that psychological disorders are rooted in the mind rather than the body, and that sexual urges and behavior are worthy of study.[3]

In 1927, Russian scientist Ivan Pavlov's study of the role of salivation in digestion led him to the discovery of what came to be known as classical or Pavlovian conditioning, which identified that learning can be a passive, unconscious process. Pavlov's research was the foundation of John Watson's theory of behaviorism, which ultimately became the leading school of experimental psychology during the mid-twentieth century. Rejecting the focus of early psychologists on introspection and consciousness, Watson called in 1913 for a complete overhaul of the science of psychology. His goal: to establish psychology as a "purely objective experimental branch of natural science" with a theoretical focus on "the prediction and control of behavior."[4]

One of the best-known experimental behaviorists was B. F. Skinner. Through his experiments on rats and pigeons, he developed a method of learning called operant conditioning in which researchers administer punishment or rewards to discourage or encourage particular behaviors, respectively. Behaviorists described a manipulation and measured an actual behavior. A manipulation might involve different probabilities of a reward, which might be a food pellet for a rat or a cookie for a child.

Because the decision-making processes occurring inside our minds are not observable, behaviorists did not view them as part of the scientific process. From the behaviorists' perspective, we can't know for certain why a rat or a person will avoid touching an object that is known to administer an electric shock; we only know that once the shock is administered, the object is avoided. As we will see, contemporary psychologists have developed methodologies to more deeply assess the cognitive reasons for the behavior—essentially by gathering new forms of data. For example, psychologists are increasingly collecting physiological measures to gather more objective evidence of participants' reactions to stimuli, such as measuring cortisol to assess stress levels and testosterone to measure aggression. The growth of brain imaging technology, including functional magnetic resonance images, has also transformed psychology experiments in profound ways. These approaches have been important innovations within the field and show all experimentalists that new data sources and approaches to data collection can yield new insight. Much as experimenters in psychology labs have sought new data such as brain imaging, companies and governments have explored new data to help evaluate the results of experiments that they are running.

Social psychology, or the empirical study of how other people influence our thoughts, feelings, and actions, became prominent in the 1930s as pioneering Jewish social psychologists fleeing the Nazis, such as Kurt Lewin, settled at US universities. Lewin's assertion that a person's behavior is a function of the person in their environment, inspired by the discrimination and danger he had faced in Europe, had an enormous influence on the experiments of well-known social psychologists such as Stanley Milgram and Philip Zimbardo.

Some of these researchers' experiments, on topics such as conformity and obedience to authority, grew out of a desire to make sense of Nazi atrocities during World War II and revealed the dark side of human behavior. For example, Milgram began his famous obedience-to-authority experiments in July 1961, three months after the start of the trial of Nazi war criminal Adolf Eichmann, to test the extent to which ordinary people would obey orders to physically harm other people. As the ordinary men Milgram had recruited arrived at his Yale University lab (at the time, Yale was still all-male), they met an experimenter and another participant, who was actually a confederate. (In psych lingo, a confederate is an actor that the experimenter has tasked with playing a role in the experiment, unbeknownst to the participants being studied.) To this day, psychology experiments are known for their frequent use of deception to simulate a situation that would otherwise be difficult to create.

In Milgram's experiments, the unknowing participant was assigned the role of "teacher," and the confederate was assigned the role of "learner." The teacher and learner then were placed in separate rooms, and the teacher was given a sample electric shock to experience what the learner might receive during the experiment. The teacher then was given word pairs to teach to the learner, who would respond by pressing a button. If the learner answered incorrectly, the experimenter instructed the teacher to give him a shock and was told that the voltage would increase incrementally with each wrong answer. In fact, no actual shocks were administered, but the teacher heard his learner (actually sounds played on a tape recorder) react with increasing distress to the alleged shocks, first crying out, then banging on the wall, and then, in some cases, complaining about his heart condition.

At this point, many in the role of teacher showed signs of distress and asked to stop the experiment and check on the learner. The experimenter simply promised the teachers that they would not be held responsible for the learner's condition and urged them to continue. Though increasingly agitated and upset, most of the teachers chose to continue administering what appeared to be agonizing shocks, even after learners fell into an ominous silence in the other room. In fact, contrary to the predictions of psychiatrists and laypeople, who expected teachers to resist giving large shocks, 65% of them administered the experiment's final allegedly massive shock of 450 volts.[5] The experiments proved controversial: Milgram was criticized for subjecting his participants to an unacceptable level of emotional stress and for allegedly failing to clearly communicate that the shocks had not been real; evidence also emerged that many of the participants suspected the shocks were faked, casting doubt on the findings.[6]

In 1971, Stanford professor Philip Zimbardo (Milgram's high school friend) recruited 18 Stanford students for a two-week study. Nine of them were unexpectedly "arrested" and taken to a mock prison in the basement of the psychology building, where they were stripped, searched, shaved, deloused, issued uniforms and ID numbers, and taken to "cells" by nine other students, who were assigned the role of "guard." The guards, who were given whistles and armed with nightsticks, were told they could treat the prisoners however they wanted, short of administering corporal punishment.

At first the prisoners mocked the guards, but as the guards began demanding obedience and inflicting punishment, such as exercise, to show their authority, conflicts broke out. On the morning of the second day, the prisoners rebelled, ripping off their uniforms and blockading themselves in their cells. The guards burst into the cells by shooting off fire extinguishers, trashed the cells, and put the prisoners who had started the rebellion in solitary confinement. The experiment grew increasingly chaotic and disturbing, with some prisoners breaking down and one even going on a hunger strike. Zimbardo himself admitted later that he came to identify with his role of "prison superintendent" and overlooked the suffering of the prisoners as a consequence. But after five days, he ended the experiment prematurely and expressed remorse for letting the situation get out of hand.[7]

Although the results chillingly suggest that ordinary human beings may be more inclined to sink to the level of their aversive circumstances than to rise above them, the experiment was widely criticized, both for its flawed methodology (including Zimbardo's participation in the study and the lack of clear independent and dependent variables) and for its inhumane treatment of its subjects.

Many of the early experiments in social psychology, including Milgram's and Zimbardo's, would no longer be allowed. Institutional review boards (IRBs) sprang up in the United States in the 1970s to protect human test subjects from physical and psychological harm. IRBs, now effectively required by law in the university context, review research plans and conduct risk-benefit analysis to determine whether to approve an experiment. Specifically, IRBs review the ethics and methods of a planned experiment, seek to maximize participant safety, and ask for evidence that subjects' participation will be voluntary and fully informed—though there are often exemptions for informed consent.

When devising an experiment, organizations need to consider the potential stress and harm that the experiment could impose on participants. The experiment may not be at risk of damaging people psychologically, but there's still a risk of implementing a change that could leave some people worse off for the duration of the experiment—all for learning's sake. Whenever decision makers are considering a change, it's important to have explicit discussions of the potential risks and harm involved. The bigger the change and potential harm, the more important the discussion. Of course, this applies to any organizational change, not just those linked to experiments. But the process of experimenting gives organizations an additional point at which to pause and think carefully both about the need and potential for learning and the potential for harm that may come from the changes they are making.

Ideally, any changes imposed will be beneficial—both for participants and for society. Returning to the history of psychological experimentation, policymakers have increasingly cited experimental results to enact social change. In the 1954 *Brown v. Board of Education of Topeka, Kansas* case, the US Supreme Court cited the 1939 and 1940 "doll studies" of husband-and-wife psychologists Mamie and Kenneth Clark as evidence that racial segregation in public schools was detrimental to African American children and should be declared unconstitutional. The psychologists presented black pre-school children, some at segregated and some at integrated schools, with a white and a black doll. The children were asked which doll they wanted to play with, which doll they thought looked "bad," which was a "nice color," and so on. All the children, but especially those in segregated schools, showed a clear preference for the white doll, evidence that they had internalized racism and (in the case of the black children) self-hatred.[8]

More recently, implicit attitudes about race (and gender) were explored in greater depth in research spearheaded by Mahzarin Banaji and Tony Greenwald. Using a tool administered via computer called the Implicit Associations Test (IAT), they found evidence that when we first see or meet someone, our minds automatically activate stereotypes of the person's race, sex, and age.[9] In the IAT, the experimental participant is instructed to categorize items that appear on the screen as quickly as possible by striking certain keys on the keyboard. The items that appear might come from one of four categories, such as "White," "Black," "Good," and "Bad." If you were shown a series of pictures of people's faces, you might be asked to press one key to indicate that the face belongs to a "Black" person and to press a different key to indicate that the face belongs to a "White" person. You would also be shown words such as "Hate," "Love," "Kill," and "Heal," which you would have to categorize by pressing the key for "Good" or the key for "Bad." In later rounds, "White" faces and "Bad" words belong to the same category and should be categorized using the same key; meanwhile, "Black" faces and "Good" words belong to the same category and should be categorized using the same key. In other rounds, "White" faces are to be paired with "Good" words, and "Black" faces with "Bad" words. Nosek, Banaji, and Greenwald report that roughly three-quarters of the

white Americans who visit their website (http://implicit.harvard
.edu; we encourage you to visit this site and participate in an IAT
test yourself) exhibit implicit pro-white attitudes. That is, they perform the stereotypic grouping (white/good; black/bad) faster than
the nonstereotypic grouping (black/good; white/bad).[10] People
who believe they don't discriminate based on race often are disap-
pointed to find that their IAT results reveal biased implicit attitudes.

Banaji has called the prevalence of these attitudes "ordinary
prejudice"—ordinary because ordinary mental processes are
involved in expressions of stereotypes and prejudice, and ordinary students and professionals will demonstrate them.[11] The IAT
has emerged as one of the most visible new technologies to experimentally study cognitive processes of which participants are often
unaware. Organizations have used the IAT to help them grapple
with and overcome their biases. According to Banaji, many organizations she has interacted with accept the premise that prejudice
occurs in the world, but view their own organization as unbiased—
until they administer the IAT to their personnel.

The IAT is a simple test that explains only a small amount of
variation in real-world decisions, but it has been enormously influential. Tens of millions of people have taken versions of the test at
implicit.harvard.edu, and the concept of implicit bias has entered
the popular culture. The evidence suggests that we can be biased
without being aware of it, and this knowledge has changed the dialogue on gender and race in contemporary society.

In other contexts, psychologists have explored different technologies and methodological approaches to better understand decision making. For example, physiological measures have become an
increasingly common way to gather more objective evidence of participants' reactions to stimuli, such as measuring cortisol to assess
stress levels and testosterone to measure aggression. The growth
of brain imaging technology, including functional magnetic resonance images, has also transformed psychology experiments in

profound ways. As psychology departments have focused on underlying bodily activity, many of the more applied experimentalists are taking jobs in professional schools within universities (such as business, law, medicine, and policy schools), in government, and in the private sector.

Experimental and Behavioral Economics

While psychologists were pioneering the use of lab experiments to understand the details of human decision making, economists were pushing the frontier in analyzing causal relationships in the field. In an influential 1983 article in the *American Economic Review*, economist Edward Leamer argued for the need for more rigorous empirical work in the field. "Hardly anyone takes data analysis seriously," he asserted.[12] Economists came around to Leamer's view, and in the decades since his critique, the field has changed dramatically. Economists did what economists often do—they looked to other fields for methods that they could adopt and adapt for the purpose of better understanding economic activity. Most notably, borrowing from the field of statistics, economists began to develop a toolkit to make causal claims about the economy. And while much of this focused on working with nonexperimental data, it also included the experimental method.

Two important early movements sprang up to incorporate experimental methods into economics. The first uses massive field experiments to shed light on the effects of actual or potential government policies, ranging from a negative income tax to free health insurance. The second is the rise of behavioral and (lab) experimental economics.

The first effort was driven in no small part by ambitious graduate students who were unconstrained by (or perhaps just blithely unaware of) the norms of the field. In 1967, for example, an MIT economics PhD student named Heather Ross set out to understand[13] whether low-income people would work less if the government provided subsidies to them instead of collecting taxes from them. After the Office of Equal Opportunity accepted her proposal, the New Jersey Income Maintenance Experiment was born; it selected low-income families to receive supplemental income when their income fell below a certain threshold. On the other side of Cambridge, Massachusetts, Harvard University doctoral student Joe Newhouse led a $300 million experiment from 1974 to 1982 that randomly selected uninsured Americans and provided them with health insurance, varying the coinsurance rates. Part of an era of grand social experiments, these initiatives were ambitious, expensive, and insightful. They were also managerially and technically complicated. For example, Newhouse's experiment involved a large team of researchers from different disciplines, specializing in areas ranging from health policy to statistical methods (the project was so complicated that it required new methods to be developed as it went along). Newhouse went on to become one of the founders of the field of health economics and is now a professor at Harvard University. And nearly fifty years after the project was run, the results from this experiment still inform our understanding of the economics of insurance and are frequently cited by academics, policymakers, and the media alike.

While we would like to see more experiments of this grand ambition, they were and continue to be rare—although they have come to play a larger role in policy. Organizations such as Mathematica Policy Research (which supported Ross's work) and the RAND Corporation (which supported Newhouse's) continue to conduct impressive experiments, but most companies and governments are still developing the know-how and foresight needed to run experiments of this magnitude. At the same time, these experiments foreshadowed the current experimental revolution in economics, which has been facilitated by a rapid rise in data availability and a dramatic decline in the cost of experimentation.

While Ross and Newhouse were leading a movement of policy experiments, a second movement was occurring within academia: the rise of behavioral and experimental economics. This led to the development of a new toolkit and a taste for experiments that could help to shed light on economic principles.

The earliest lab experiments generally sought to test economic theories by exploring the extent to which human behavior reflects the predictions of economic models. This work used lab experiments on human subjects, a method that had been used in psychology. As early as 1948, Harvard professor Edward Chamberlin experimentally tested the neoclassical theory of perfect competition, using experiments to help identify areas where existing economic theories were and weren't sufficient.[14] In 1959, German economists Heinz Sauermann and Reinhard Selten (the latter of whom won a Nobel Prize in 1994) published experimental studies of price formation in oligopolies (markets with a small number of providers who create limited competition).[15]

Early game theorists also tested their models with simple experiments in the 1950s, and psychologist Sidney Siegel and economist Lawrence E. Fouraker used experiments to study bargaining behavior in the early 1960s.[16] Experimental tests allowed economists to test and extend the theories that dominated the field. These experiments accounted for a miniscule fraction of economics research but were harbingers of changes to come.

One person credited with bringing experiments into the mainstream of economics is Vernon Smith, who was awarded the Nobel Prize in Economics in 2002 for this achievement (a prize he shared with psychologist Daniel Kahneman). Working in the 1960s and '70s, Smith, a student of Chamberlin's, not only made important early contributions to the field but led and advised a generation of younger economists who heavily influenced the development of experimental economics. Smith's specific contributions lie in the area of alternative market mechanisms (different types of auctions), and his methodological contributions include developing well-accepted methods for creating markets in the lab. Within the market mechanisms that Smith studied, trading prices that emerged between buyers and sellers in experiments typically came very close to the theoretical equilibrium—that is, rationally predicted—price; thus, his work supported a belief in rational decision making.

Smith was also a key figure in creating the rules that governed what constituted good evidence in experimental economics.[17] Smith's influence highlights that social scientists in different fields have adopted different definitions of rationality and different standards for determining whether people's behavior is rational. More importantly, different fields came to different conclusions about what made for a good experiment and about how to interpret results.

At the time, psychologists often examined the hypothetical decisions of subjects without providing them with monetary incentives, sometimes deceived subjects when studying social contexts, and studied one-shot decisions that did not provide the opportunity to learn across trials. In addition, psychologists most commonly used the term "rationality" to refer to the actions of the individual rather than the outcomes of markets. Smith developed experimental methods that were at times more specific and rigid than the approach of psychology. For example, subjects often received monetary incentives that would vary with performance on a task, with the goal of helping participants to better understand the "rules of the game." Experimental economists also generally sought to avoid deceiving participants, in contrast to work in social psychology—where deception was the norm.

And while Herbert Simon clearly thought first about the rationality of the individual, Smith focused on the market and how it evolved across a large number of experimental trials. If early rounds of an experiment did not achieve the outcomes predicted by models of rational behavior, Smith did not perceive this to be a problem. And if some study participants made terrible decisions and went broke but the market still reached equilibrium, many economists took this as evidence that existing theories provided reasonable descriptions of markets as a whole.

George Loewenstein, a prominent behavioral economist who has conducted many influential experiments, has expressed concern about economics' early limited focus on markets across repeated trials. "Such markets have remarkable efficiency properties; they converge to equilibrium," he writes. "They do so, in part, by ... eliminating the influence of participants who behave in a suboptimal fashion." That is, by focusing on markets, economists found a convenient way to confirm their belief in the rationality of human decision making in their experiments, Loewenstein argues. He cynically comments on the rigid rules and highly formal structure of the experiments that Smith and his colleagues designed: "The last time I participated in *any* type of auction was as a teenager when I bought a broken washing machine motor for $0.25. Most of the economic transactions that I, and probably most people, participate in, whether large or small, are notable for the lack of disciplinary mechanisms."[18] Similarly, Colin Camerer—another leading behavioral economist—playfully criticizes the constraining nature of Smith's rules by comparing the subjects in traditional experimental economics, forced to repeat trials over and over, to the Bill Murray character in the film *Groundhog Day*, who must relive the same day again and again until he gets it right.[19] It is important to note that Camerer and Loewenstein themselves often conducted research within some of the precise parameters laid down by Smith. But like many leading members of the next generation of economists, they had no problem relaxing these rules to pursue their scientific question of interest.

Behind this seemingly esoteric squabble between two academic disciplines, there is an important lesson for experimentalists everywhere: there is no single perfect way to run an experiment. Determining your approach to experimentation depends on the question you are asking. When asked about the research of Smith and that of Daniel Kahneman (whose work we'll soon explore further), another Nobel winner, Al Roth (whose work we will also discuss shortly), was quick to note: "Kahneman's a psychologist—he's interested in how your brain works, how you make decisions. Smith is an economist. He's interested in how markets work." This distinction can help to explain the different rules that govern the implementation of experiments in the two fields.

For organizations, it also underscores the importance of thinking carefully about the question you are trying to answer before designing an experiment. For example, suppose that Amazon was experimenting with different layouts of its website. Should it play by the rules of psychology (if a user has difficulty navigating the site on her first try, then it's clear the design has serious flaws) or the rules of economics (wait until a user has had several interactions with the site before deciding whether the new design is easier or harder to use)? The answer depends on Amazon's goal, how often the consumer will experience the site, and factors such as the extent to which Amazon is worried about users leaving the platform immediately versus trying to curate better experiences over the long haul, in which case a short-term blip might be less important. (Of course, a number of other factors would come into play as well—which is exactly the point.)

As economists became increasingly interested in using experiments for different goals than psychologists, and in testing the behavioral assumptions underlying economic theory, economic research methods evolved accordingly. As the field developed, many experimental economists in the generation that followed Smith found that an orthodox adherence to his rules prevented some of their results from being of interest to the broader economics community. If their experimental data didn't confirm the market-level predictions of existing models, they complained, many reviewers of economics journals would argue there was something wrong with their methods or interpretation. This barrier started to come down only after decades had passed since Smith formalized the rules of economic experimentation. In 1999, Loewenstein wrote, "It is easy to forget that only 20 years ago the simple fact that an article reported experiments or discussed psychology was regarded by many editors as grounds for summary rejection." Thus, Smith ushered in the use of experiments in economics, yet his rules may have delayed psychology's influence on economics.

That influence took a leap forward with the research partnership of Al Roth and Keith Murnighan. When he joined the University of Illinois faculty in 1974, Roth was a mathematically gifted young game theorist. As he mentioned in his 2012 Nobel Prize paper, when he went to Illinois he was primarily known for proving "a fixed point theorem on lattices." If you don't know what that means, don't worry—you're not alone.[20] Roth's interests considerably broadened when he met Murnighan, who was also starting his first faculty position at Illinois after receiving a PhD in social psychology at Purdue. At the time, an operations-researcher-turned-economist and a social psychologist would typically only cross paths at a social function, or as the start of a bad joke. But an insightful senior colleague, playing academic matchmaker, introduced them to each other and suggested they chat about research. They did. Ultimately, the world would benefit from the exciting collaborations that followed. "Experiments were newer to me than game theory was to him," Roth later recalled of his partnership with Murnighan, "but over the course of the next decade we taught each other how to do experiments that would say something useful about game theory."[21]

The pair would go on to write a dozen papers together that expanded the possibilities of what economic experiments could be.

Their papers formally analyzed what rational actors would do in economic games, often focusing on games that had more than one equilibrium—that is, multiple possible results that could emerge from fully rational actors. In their view, other social sciences, such as psychology and sociology, had the potential to enlighten the field of economics about which economic solution would emerge when multiple rational options were available. Most importantly, they used sociological and psychological concepts to explain how their study participants departed from rationally predicted outcomes. This series of papers was rigorous in its specification of what economic models predicted and was rooted in formal economic theories, yet provided accurate and insightful descriptions of actual behavior based on psychology and sociology. As such, Murnighan and Roth may have become the first behavioral economists well before the field of behavioral economics, or even the term itself, existed.

Roth and Murnighan's experimental insights included:

- Game-theoretic models do a pretty good job of explaining behavior, but actual behavior departs from purely rational behavior in systematic ways.
- What each side knows about the other (asymmetry of information) and communication structure are critical determinants of bargaining outcomes.
- The likelihood of a relationship continuing between two (or more) people has important effects on the likelihood that they will cooperate with one another.
- While being risk averse leads bargainers to make concessions to resolve their aversion, in predictable contexts this is less harmful than economic models predict.

Overall, Roth and Murnighan helped to lay the groundwork for the fruitful collaborations between economics and the other social sciences that would follow. Recently, Roth talked to us about this work and, more broadly, about the power and limitations of experiments. During the conversation, it became clear to us that many of the lessons he has learned and developed in the context of lab experiments are equally relevant in the field. For example, he mentioned that he is very careful to talk about "series of experiments" because he thinks that multiple experiments are more likely than one single experiment to answer a complete question. He also talked about generalizability, namely the challenge of generalizing the result of a lab experiment to the field, but also from one field context to another. For example, should we believe that an incentive experiment that varies wages for line cooks would tell us anything more about incentives offered to elite athletes than a lab experiment would? Roth noted that similar experiments in different field settings have generated effects in opposite directions. And he talked about how participants can learn across rounds of an experiment—and the importance of making sure participants know what they are supposed to be doing. These lessons are valuable not only for lab experimenters but for managers who are running experiments.

Economics Meets Psychology

The work of Roth and Murnighan foreshadowed a new wave of experimental economics, as well as the incorporation of psychological insights into economic models. Among the most impressive results was a body of Nobel prize-winning work conducted by Daniel Kahneman and Amos Tversky. The pair's famous research collaboration has been covered extensively by journalist Michael Lewis in his excellent book *The Undoing Project* and by Kahneman himself in his bestseller *Thinking, Fast and Slow*. Both books focus on the men's friendship and their notable influence on the fields of psychology and economics. We recommend both, if you haven't read them.

But Kahneman and Tversky had another notable achievement that has gotten much less attention: they laid the groundwork for the creation of the field of behavioral economics. Ultimately, they lit the spark that led to the rise of behavioral insights groups around the globe and the proliferation of the types of behavioral experiments that organizations are now putting into practice. Here's how.

As we've noted, until the 1970s, the fields of psychology and economics developed largely in isolation from each other. Initially, Tversky and Kahneman were operating squarely (and successfully) in the domain of psychology. They devised experiment after experiment that compellingly and brilliantly identified a variety of systematic errors in judgment and decision making.

The pair's paradigm-shifting 1974 *Science* paper, "Judgment under Uncertainty: Heuristics and Biases," showed that people aren't as rational as traditional economic models often assumed. Tversky and Kahneman identified heuristics, or cognitive rules of thumb, that people use to make decisions quickly and efficiently. For example, they defined the availability heuristic as the tendency of people to assess the frequency, probability, or likely causes of an event by the degree to which instances of that event are readily available in memory. And, according to the representativeness heuristic, when making a judgment about an individual, object, or event, people tend to look for traits that correspond with stereotypes they've previously formed.

This work kicked off the development of a rich literature uncovering the systematic ways in which humans depart from rationality and provided the springboard for what is now called behavioral economics. Other fields, including marketing, negotiations, and medical decision making, started to take note and to incorporate the potential for systematic bias into their worldviews.

While Kahneman and Tversky's ideas were very influential in some domains, it was their next line of work that captured the attention of economists. In a paper called "Prospect Theory: An Analysis of Decisions under Risk" published in *Econometrica*, a leading economics journal catering to the most hardcore economists, they developed a mathematical model in the language of economics that challenged the field's core assumptions of rationality. Kahneman and Tversky's ambition was clear from the first sentence of the abstract: "This paper presents a critique of expected utility theory as a descriptive model of decision making under risk, and develops an alternative model, called prospect theory." The gloves were off.

Economists took note. Some economists loved prospect theory; others hated it. Some argued that it was a better predictor of behavior than the standard expected utility model; others argued that it was worse. A 2004 paper by economist John List argued that the answer depends on the situation and the question of interest. Looking at participants in a sports card trading show, he found that people with less market experience acted in ways that were more consistent with prospect theory, while those with more experience in the marketplace behaved in a way that was more consistent with the standard economic model.

Although prospect theory did not become the new standard model of economics, it did leave the field with the important realization that human behavior deviates from the traditional model in important ways. Kahneman and Tversky's work has also become an exemplar of the influence of psychology and behavioral economics on some experiments being run in organizations.

Consider the following thought experiment, developed by Kahneman and Tversky in a 1981 paper:

> Imagine that the United States is preparing for the outbreak of an unusual Asian disease that is expected to kill 600 people. Two alternative programs to combat the disease have been proposed. Assume that exact scientific estimates of the consequences of the programs are as follows.
> *Program A*: If Program A is adopted, 200 people will be saved.
> *Program B*: If Program B is adopted, there is a one-third probability that 600 people will be saved and a two-thirds probability that no people will be saved.
> Which of the two programs would you favor?

There are a number of factors you might consider when evaluating these options in the real world. For example, what will be the impact of each program on the broader society? Who is most at risk for the disease? Which option would provide the greatest benefit? But if you had to pick Program A or Program B based only on the information given in the problem, which program would you choose? Most people choose Program A.

Let's consider how you might think through this decision. One simple rule for making decisions is always to select the alternative with the highest expected value—the strategy that provides the best outcome, on average. But, as you can see, in this case the expected values of the two programs are equal. Program A will definitely save 200 lives. Program B has a one-third chance of saving 600 lives or, on average, will save 200 lives.

Now consider a second version of the Asian Disease Problem, also from the 1981 paper:

> Imagine that the United States is preparing for the outbreak of
> an unusual Asian disease that is expected to kill 600 people. Two
> alternative programs to combat the disease have been proposed.
> Assume that the scientific estimates of the consequences of the
> programs are as follows.
> Program C: If Program C is adopted, 400 people will die.
> Program D: If Program D is adopted, there is a one-third
> probability that no one will die and a two-thirds probability that
> 600 people will die.
> Which of the two programs would you favor?

You've probably noticed that the two sets of programs are objectively the same. Saving 200 people (Program A) offers the same objective outcome as losing 400 people (Program C), and programs B and D are also objectively identical. However, most individuals choose Program A in the first set and Program D in the second set.[22]

While the two sets of choices are objectively identical, the framing of outcomes in terms of lives saved versus lives lost is sufficient to shift the most common response from risk-averse to risk-seeking behavior. Kahneman and Tversky used the term *framing* to refer to alternative wordings of the same objective information. Their work demonstrates a simple but important point: framing matters.

Kahneman and Tversky's concept of framing has been used to help explain real-world situations where people react differently to risks framed as gains than to those framed as losses. For example, in one paper, economist Devin Pope found that professional golfers are more likely to leave their putts short when shooting for birdies as compared to shooting for par.[23] One potential explanation of this finding is that golfers feel more pressure to avoid bogeys (where a bogey might feel like a loss) than to get birdies (which feel more like a gain relative to par).

More recently, organizations have also used experiments to see where and how they can use framing effects to their advantage. For example, economists Roland Fryer, Steven Levitt, John List, and Sally Sadoff teamed up with nine schools in the Chicago suburb of Chicago Heights to figure out whether they could harness the power of framing in a teacher incentive program. The researchers randomly assigned a set of teachers to one of two incentive packages, one with a gain frame and the other with a loss frame. In the gain frame, teachers were promised a bonus at end of the year if their students met prespecified performance targets. In the loss frame, teachers were given the same bonus for having their students meet the same targets—but with a twist. Instead of getting the bonus at the end of the year, they were given it upfront and told that they would have to repay it at the end of the year if students failed to meet targets. The team found that the loss-frame contract, but not the gain-frame contract, led to large gains in math scores.[24]

While the study by Fryer and colleagues changed more than the framing, it does highlight the ways in which organizations are incorporating insights from behavioral economics and psychology, as well as the role experiments are playing in figuring out what works in different contexts. Without the experiment, it would be hard to know how effective the incentive package's structure would be at meeting its goals.

Behavioral Economics Emerges as a Field

In 1977, Richard Thaler and Daniel Kahneman met while visiting Stanford University. Kahneman had already changed the field of psychology and laid the groundwork to transform economics. Thaler was a new assistant professor who was trying to find his way, his path toward tenure (let alone the Nobel Prize he would eventually win) still unclear. (We spoke with a classmate from his PhD program, who recalls wondering whether Thaler would even be able to graduate from the program!) Kahneman helped to set Thaler on a new path—one that would change his life and lead to the emergence of behavioral economics. In the process, Thaler became excited about psychology and the way it can shape our understanding of economics.

Like Kahneman and Tversky, Thaler had a knack for asking questions that would get to the heart of assumptions of economics that didn't fit existing theories. In a 1980 paper, he asked people to think about the following scenarios:

- Mr. R bought a case of good wine in the late 1950s for about $5 a bottle. A few years later, the wine merchant offered to buy the wine back for $100 a bottle. Mr. R refused, although he has never paid more than $35 for a bottle of wine.

- Mr. H mows his own lawn. His neighbor's son would mow it for $8. But although Mr. H mows his own lawn, he wouldn't mow his neighbor's same-sized lawn for $20.

- A family pays $40 for tickets to a basketball game to be played 60 miles from their home. On the day of the game, there is a snowstorm. They decide to go anyway, but note in passing that had the tickets been given to them, they would have stayed home.[25]

Most people identify with these everyday decisions, recognizing them as ones they might make themselves. Yet from the perspective of standard economic theory, the behavior or thoughts of those in each scenario depart from rationality. The value you place on the wine, time, labor, or basketball tickets in a snowstorm should not be affected by whether or not you already own them. In contrast, as Thaler's vignettes suggest, our actual decision-making processes depart from the rational logic predicted by standard economic theory.

Thaler gained visibility in economics with a column he published in the *Journal of Economic Perspectives* from 1987 to 1990 entitled "Anomalies." Each column would highlight one systematic departure that people make from rational behavior, in violation of the assumptions of traditional microeconomic theory. The journal was highly visible to the economics community, the articles were very well written, and Thaler was canny about identifying which anomalies would be convincing to economists. Many of these anomalies had been identified through experimentation (which was still a new tool within economics), and the column served to highlight both the emerging field of behavioral economics and the informative power of experiments.

Along with Roth, Smith, Kahneman, and Tversky, Thaler was central to alerting economists to the breakthroughs they could achieve by running experiments. Their work helped to inspire a generation of leading scholars, including George Loewenstein, Colin Camerer, David Laibson, Linda Babcock, Iris Bohnet, Matthew Rabin, and Sendhil Mullainathan, all of whom would lean heavily on the experimental method and bring psychology to core problems in economics.

Behavioral economics has played a special role in laying the groundwork for the behavioral policy experiments that have proliferated over the past decade. In particular, Thaler's 2008 book *Nudge*, cowritten with the prominent legal scholar Cass Sunstein, helped to inspire the creation of the Behavioural Insights Team, which we described in chapter 1. BIT, in turn, has inspired a broader behavioral insights movement in policy settings. Simply put: without Kahneman and Tversky, it's hard to imagine Thaler doing the path-breaking work he's done. And without his work, and the broader growth of behavioral economics, it's hard to imagine behavioral policy experiments gaining as much traction in practice as they have.

The Rise of Field Experiments

While Thaler was off creating the field of behavioral economics, other branches of economics were also learning about experiments. As we've mentioned, some of the early economics experiments aimed at evaluating social policies were launched on a large scale—predating the birth of behavioral economics and experimental economics as fields. Since then, economists have increasingly worked with companies and governments to run experiments.

In recent decades, economists have run experiments in areas ranging from health to labor to marketing, focusing on issues ranging from the impact of health insurance to tests of behavioral economics theories. Many of these experiments have been field experiments—that is, they have been run outside of the lab. While some of them essentially look like lab experiments but in a field setting, others are experiments in which participants are just going about their business and don't even know that they are in an experiment. Within economics, this type of field experiment is often referred to as a natural field experiment, a term coined by economists Glenn Harrison and John List (who helped to popularize field experiments within economics).[26]

Perhaps no branch of economics has been more transformed by field experiments than development economics, an area that focuses on understanding and improving fiscal, economic, and social conditions in developing countries. In 1994, economist Michael Kremer helped to kickstart the use of experiments among development economists and practitioners alike when he set out to answer a simple but important question: Does giving new textbooks to schools in Kenya improve educational outcomes?[27] This is a context in which looking at the cross-sectional correlation can be misleading. After all, schools with textbooks might well have access to other important drivers of education as well (such as more engaged parents or better teachers).

To understand the causal impact of the book program, Kremer and his collaborators ran an experiment in which a randomly selected subset of Kenyan primary schools were given textbooks (by a Dutch nonprofit) while other schools were not. The answer was more nuanced than previous research that relied on nonexperimental data had suggested: Textbooks seemed to have some positive effect on test scores, but only for students who were already top performers at their school.[28] Kremer and others went on to experimentally test other ways to improve student outcomes, ranging from investing in student health to providing school uniforms. This body of work has helped to provide frameworks for organizations that are trying to figure out how best to invest in education.[29]

The past two decades have seen a broad and dramatic shift toward experiments throughout development economics, both in research and in practice. The Abdul Latif Jameel Poverty Action Lab, or J-PAL, has been a central driver of this change. J-PAL was founded in 2003 by Abhijit Banerjee, Esther Duflo, and Sendhil Mullainathan, all MIT economists at the time, to promote the use of randomized control trials to enable more effective evaluations of development policy—and a better understanding of how to improve wellbeing around the world. J-PAL sought to reduce poverty by ensuring that policy is informed by scientific evidence, primarily the use of field experiments. Currently led by Banerjee, Duflo, Rachel Glennerster, and Benjamin Olken, J-PAL coordinates a network of 145 affiliated professors from 49 universities who provide research, outreach, and training around the world on effective poverty reduction interventions. As of February 2018, J-PAL affiliates had conducted over 850 randomized control trials in 80 countries.

Other branches of economics are experiencing similar transformations. Virtually every field of economics now uses field experiments, from labor economics to industrial organization to marketing to health economics. While experiments are far from the only tool being used, they have become an important one. Field experiments—often conducted with companies, governments, or NGOs—have sowed the seeds of experimentation in sector after sector, as organizations have benefited not only from the substance of experimental results but also from a broader appreciation of the value of experimentation.

3
The Rise of Behavioral Experiments in Policymaking

In the United States, over 100,000 people are on waiting lists for organs. More than one-third of them will die before an organ is found, and only about 30,000 will get an organ this year—often from someone who has died and chose to donate their organs. This policy issue is literally a matter of life and death.

To facilitate organ donations, governments often have a system allowing people to become an organ donor after their death. The government then has an important choice about how to design the system. They can assume you do not want to be a donor, and require you to fill out a form (or check a box) if you want to become a donor—this is an "opt in" system. Or they can assume you want to be a donor, and require you to fill out a form (or check a box) to opt *out* of being a donor. In many US states, for example, you have to expressly agree to donate your organs upon death by filling out a form if you want to be an organ donor; otherwise medical personnel will assume you want to keep them in your body.

An influential 2003 paper by Eric Johnson and Dan Goldstein suggests that opt-in and opt-out policies might lead to very different organ donation rates. Looking at eleven European countries, the authors found that the four with opt-in systems had organ donations rates between 4% and 28%, while the seven with opt-out systems had donation rates ranging from 86% to 100%.[1] The defaults seem to be playing an important role in the donation rates.

As a result, the decision about whether to make organ donation registries opt-in or opt-out has become a contentious policy issue. While fans of an opt-out system point to the potential to save lives, critics worry about people who don't want to be donors but never get around to opting out. According to a report by the US Department of Health and Human Services, the results of a 2012 survey showed about 47% of respondents opposing the policy. When people opposing presumed consent were asked why, the most common response was that "it should be the individual's decision or freedom of choice." Moreover, nearly a quarter of respondents said that they would opt out of donating under such a system.[2] Given the very low opt-out rates in presumed consent systems, it is certainly possible that some people might want to opt out but never end up doing so (though it's hard to know, without more evidence).

This has implications for the donation process after a would-be donor's death as well. In the United States, the next of kin of registered donors almost always consent to proceed with the organ donation. In an opt-out system, the signal of intent sent by being registered is much noisier, which can lead families to wonder about the true intent of a deceased family member, and potentially to refuse consent even for a registered donor.

"Active choice" has emerged as a potential alternative, with the hope of increasing donation rates while addressing some of the concerns of those who object to presumed consent.[3] In this type of system, there is no default option and people are forced to actively decide whether or not they want to be a donor. Active choice has garnered considerable support and advocacy in policy and academic circles. A variety of states ask citizens when they renew their driver's license to actively decide whether they want to consent to organ donation, and there has been a recent movement for governments to switch to this (California, New York, and the UK all recently made the switch from opt-in to active choice). There's only one problem: until recently, there had been little evidence of its effect on registration rates.

Motivated by this, economists Judd Kessler and Al Roth (Al has been a central figure in developing the system that matches donated organs with those in need) set out to investigate how people would respond to an active choice regime. They looked at data on how organ donor registration rates were evolving over time in different states, comparing changes in California (which had recently changed its policy from opt-in to active choice) to changes in other states that had not changed their policies. The data did not look promising for active choice. Whereas other states saw registration rates increase, California saw a decline in registration rates after the policy.[4]

An experiment was in order. The pair recruited 368 people with Massachusetts licenses and brought them into the lab to make real-world decisions about whether to switch their donor status (participants did not know the topic of the experiment until they arrived). To get this ambitious experiment up and running, Kessler and Roth went to lengths to connect their laboratory computers to the Massachusetts Registry of Motor Vehicles online database so that they could record people's actual decisions about whether to switch their donor status. Participants logged onto the computers through a web interface that the researchers designed in which participants interacted with the real Massachusetts Organ and Tissue Donor Registry. The researchers then varied the way in which the choice was displayed. Some participants were in an opt-in regime, while others were asked to make an active choice. As it turns out, active choice turned out to be ineffective—in fact, fewer people signed up to be a donor in the active choice system than in the opt-in one.

The experiment was ambitious, creative, and complicated to pull off, but ultimately was fruitful in providing compelling evidence that speaks to an important ongoing policy debate. The results provide an eye-opening reminder of the ways in which we often rely on intuition when making decisions and of the role that experiments can play in complementing intuition and informing policy and managerial decisions. While there is certainly more work to be done in this area, the experiment reinforces both the need to consider carefully how to think about decision making (and defaults in particular) and the need to be cautious about promoting one system over another before the evidence is in.

Recent work by psychologist Julian Zlatev (our colleague at Harvard) and his colleagues looked more broadly at the use of default settings and found that inaccurate beliefs might be part of a broader pattern. In a lab experiment, Zlatev found that people often do not correctly anticipate the effects of defaults and do not always use them in a way that is consistent with their goals. (People had the most trouble setting defaults when each option had pros and cons.)[5] In the context of organ donations, policy positions might be driven in part by different perceptions of what the effects of the policy change will be.

Since running the organ donation experiment, Kessler and Roth have received considerable political backlash from people who advocated active choice and were uninterested in seeing results that did not conform to their beliefs. The pair remain undeterred and are continuing to collect new data on the issue. Roth is especially used to pushback from people with vested interests. His work has helped to design better ways to match students to schools, medical students to residency programs, and organs to those in need of a transplant—and in each of these settings, there has been heated debate about whether to bring in new evidence and approaches. "It's too important to leave to politics, even academic politics," according to Roth.[6]

Like the tax letter discussed in chapter 1 and the teacher bonuses presented in chapter 2, this experiment is part of a growing area of behavioral research that experimentally tests ideas from psychology and economics in real-world contexts with the hope of identifying the factors at play in different situations.

In this chapter, we'll explain the role experiments play in adapting behavioral insights to policy settings. But first it will be helpful to provide some additional information about nudging (a sub-branch of behavioral economics that is often associated with behavioral policy experiments).

Nudging

As Richard Thaler and Cass Sunstein wrote in *Nudge: Improving Decisions about Health, Wealth, and Happiness*, the government is a choice architect—designing not only the available options but also the way they are presented. The pair urge policymakers to be thoughtful about their role as choice architect and to try to "nudge" people in a direction that would leave society better off.

In the best of worlds, nudges draw on our knowledge of people's biases to anticipate their decision-making mistakes and design systems that have the potential to correct for these mistakes. Thaler and Sunstein advocate nudges as a tool that can allow well-intentioned policymakers and managers to help improve people's decisions.[7]

The idea of choice architecture stands in stark contrast with earlier approaches to improving decision making. Whereas many behavioral economists and psychologists had been focusing on helping individuals debias themselves through more careful decision making (which continues to be an important part of the puzzle), the core idea of nudging focuses on changing the choice environment. In the case of organ donations, we saw that an opt-out default capitalizes on the status quo bias, or the tendency for people to accept things as they are: because people are unlikely to make the effort to opt out of organ donation, opt-out policies can lead to higher organ donation rates.[8]

Strategic choices of defaults have now been used in a variety of situations to opt us into or out of things ranging from mailing list subscriptions to 401k savings. Sometimes we love the defaults we're nudged into—shout-out to our employer, Harvard University, which defaults us into sensible investment choices in our retirement accounts ... err, or, at least we hope they do ... we haven't checked recently. Sometimes we're annoyed by what feels like a bait and switch—we're looking at you, credit cards that we mean to cancel but keep forgetting—leaving us with a $99 annual fee for a card we don't even use. The lesson here isn't that a specific default is or isn't a good idea. It is that defaults and other elements of the choice environment matter, so we should think carefully about how to design them. And experiments have been central in the attempt to figure out which nudges are effective in different situations.

To relate the concept of choice architecture back to the psychology of decision making, it's helpful to have a sense of an idea that psychologists call the "dual-systems" model—that is, the notion that our minds operate in two different modes. The dual-systems model that had the greatest impact on the decision-making literature was Keith Stanovich and Richard West's distinction between System 1 and System 2 cognitive functioning, a distinction that Kahneman endorsed in his Nobel Prize talk and paper and applied as an organizing framework for his book *Thinking, Fast and Slow*.[9]

The core idea is that we make most decisions in life automatically, effortlessly, and implicitly, and give strong weight to our emotional reactions. This type of thinking is System 1, our intuitive system. Occasionally, we slow down, consciously thinking through a decision and expending effort in an attempt to be logical. This is System 2 thinking. Notice that you don't have time to make every decision at the grocery store using System 2—it would take too long (trust us, we've tried; one of us spent twenty minutes comparison-shopping paper towels and ended up buying the same brand we always get, resulting in a very annoyed spouse). In most situations, our System 1 thinking is probably fine, as we are too busy to engage System 2 for most of our decisions.

The problem is that when System 1 is in control, we can be more susceptible to biased decision making. If we want people to make better decisions when they're confronting important choices, one reasonable approach is to find ways to help them to engage their System 2. This can take a wide variety of forms, from using algorithms or simple decision-making models, to asking deliberative friends, to working in groups, to simply writing down the costs and benefits of each action. Your System 1 self thinks you can put together your new grill without instructions. Your System 2 asks your family if you should bother using the instructions, and quickly realizes that the answer is yes.

In contrast, choice architecture—in its purest form—focuses on redesigning the choice environment in way that will guide people toward making better decisions. Instead of you asking your family about the instructions, your family preemptively puts the instructions next to your iced tea to make sure they are top of mind. Choice architecture ultimately transfers the debiasing process from the individual decision maker to the government or company (or family member) that is designing the choice environment to begin with.

The Nuance behind Behavioral Insights

In principle, nudges can help to address inefficiencies that abound throughout society. Yet, as we saw in the case of setting the default for organ donation registries, the implementation of nudges is rarely as simple as it seems on the surface. First, context matters—and experiments can help us figure out which set of interventions is most likely to be effective in a given setting.

Second, design choices matter. Existing frameworks rarely test the exact intervention you want to implement, and small changes in how you design a nudge can make a big impact. For example, an influential study by Hunt Alcott found that the impact of a nudge telling people that they use less energy than their neighbors depended on whether or not there was a smiley face next to the message. While this answers one design question, it raises many others, such as: what about other emojis? In practice, an organization would want to think about the broader set of design choices at their disposal, which surely won't all be analyzed by existing academic research alone.

Third, unintended consequences abound—and can also vary in different situations. For example, a large body of work has explored the impact of defaulting people into 401k plans. While this has been shown to increase savings, it also has been found to have an unintended consequence—people who were nudged to save more ended up going into more debt as well. It is probably still a good idea in aggregate to nudge people into 401k savings, but this important unintended consequence is both conceptually interesting and practically important for those looking to implement a nudge in this context. Just thinking that "defaults work" wasn't enough to act on in this situation. When putting a nudge into practice, it's important to think through both the intended and unintended consequences. We've seen plenty of well-intentioned behavioral interventions end up being ineffective, or even backfiring.

The Link between Experiments and Nudging

Thaler and Sunstein don't talk a lot about experiments in *Nudge*. Yet, in the decade since the term was coined, experiments have played a critical role in the diffusion of nudging and behavioral insights in practice. As we saw in chapter 1, behavioral insights were initially viewed with skepticism in many "serious" policy circles. Many psychologists and behavioral economists saw the use of behavioral insights in policy as a no-brainer—after all, many of the ideas on how to nudge people had already been tested in various forms in the lab (and occasionally in field settings as well). But while the lab (and a lot of the early behavioral research more broadly) have been invaluable for understanding mechanisms and creating general frameworks, some skeptical voices questioned how important these factors were in the real-world circumstances that mattered most—as mentioned above, would behavioral insights have an economically large effect on the bottom line? Of course, the answer depends on which behavioral interventions we are talking about, and which context.

By running experiments, behaviorally inclined policy wonks were able to demonstrate the value of nudging in their setting of interest, rather than rely on research that pointed to the general value of behavioral insights. In addition to improving policy outcomes, the experiments run by nudge units around the world have the additional benefit of demonstrating their own value to the shrinking set of policymakers who question whether experiments are worthwhile. As it turns out, this is one reason why organizations experiment. By having a product or service evaluated through a rigorous experiment, organizations have a much clearer picture of the value it can bring to stakeholders. Startups increasingly do this as a way of showing their value to customers and investors. And if the product or service is ineffective, then do something else that is more valuable!

Experiments have also played a central role in shaping organizations' understanding of how to design nudges and of the contexts in which they are most likely to be effective. Because of all of the nuances listed above, organizations need to experiment to refine ideas from research to put them into practice in the area they are looking to change, taking into account their specific goals. For example, like many decision-making biases identified in lab experiments, the status quo bias has been shown to be an important factor in decisions and in getting people to make different (and hopefully better) ones.[10] Yet new policy experiments continue to shed new light on how nudges might backfire and on how effective they are for solving different policy problems. Of course, you can't experiment with everything, but for now we'll reiterate this: experimentation is valuable for determining what type of intervention is likely to improve decision making in a particular context.

To best understand this issue, consider the work of Steve Levitt (of *Freakonomics* fame) and John List.[11] The pair discuss the ways in which laboratory experiments might or might not generalize to the field. While they talk a bit about whether an effect replicates at all, they more commonly argue that the *magnitude* of an effect found in the lab is often different from the magnitude of the effect in field settings. We certainly agree with this observation. It has long been recognized that laboratory experimentalists have so much control over the things they are testing that they can influence the strength of their impact on the outcome of study. Thus, lab experiments can help us know whether and when an effect might be relevant, but won't predict the exact effect in any particular real-world setting.

This challenge extends beyond the lab: the magnitude of an effect in any given field setting is also likely to be different from its magnitude in other field settings. This implies that, more generally, it can be hard to figure out how to translate findings between settings—whether from a lab or a field experiment. Our friend Al Roth once quipped that "there can at times be the misconception that there are only two settings in the world: the lab and the field." His insightful comment pointed out an obvious yet often overlooked point: context matters, and no two field settings are identical. The impact of an intervention on people's decisions will vary depending on the context. For example, signing at the top of a form might have a bigger impact on honesty for people reporting their car's mileage to their insurance agency than for people reporting their annual income (or perhaps vice versa). Similarly, people in different parts of the world may respond differently to the same nudge due to cultural differences.

In fact, this issue of generalizability highlights one of the fundamental contributions of social psychology: context matters. This is precisely why small changes in how we make decisions can have meaningful effects on our behavior. But it also means that when you read in the media or in this book about an interesting nudge, you will gain insight into a type of nudge that *might* work, but you will have more limited insight into *how much* it is likely to affect behavior in any given setting (outside of the one it was tested in). Even the directions of effects can be unpredictable. For example, emphasizing a company's mission, rather than pay, in hiring advertisements will likely affect the number of applications—but might increase or decrease applications, depending on myriad factors such as the type of job and the competitiveness of the pay.

Asking whether a nudge works is akin to asking whether advertising works. The answer for advertising is yes, for some businesses, in some situations—but in other situations, it can be ineffective or even annoying to customers. The impact of nudges is similarly nuanced. Academic research and other existing evidence can help to build general frameworks, but running their own experiments can help organizations gain an advantage by expanding these frameworks, refining and tailoring broad frameworks for a context of interest, and ultimately implementing more effective changes. And just as organizations increasingly experimentally test their advertising strategies (a topic we'll return to shortly), they can also test the choice environments they are providing to their customers, employees, and other stakeholders.

Back to the Nudge Unit

We introduced you to BIT leaders David Halpern and Owain Service in chapter 1. Both had records of public service before the British government got into the nudge business, and Halpern had been a tenured member of the psychology faculty at Cambridge. As we mentioned, after their successful revision of the tax letter in 2010, they went on to run hundreds of experiments (over 500 at this writing). They didn't invent many of the tools now common to the behavioral insights world. Nor did they create the first real-world nudges—we documented several earlier ones elsewhere in this chapter. Rather, they were skilled practitioners in using social science, combined with the logic of choice architecture, to create an organization that would work to make governments more effective and provide a model for other organizations and governments to follow. Their great innovation was twofold: putting behavioral insights into practice and helping to launch an experimental revolution within behavioral policy settings.

David Halpern was chief analyst in Tony Blair's Strategy Unit, but when David Cameron formed the Conservative–Liberal Democrat coalition government in 2010, he asked Halpern to use the tools of behavioral insights to help the government run more effectively—particularly, to save government money. BIT was formed on a probationary basis with a "sunset clause" demanding a tenfold return on the unit's costs by 2012. The initial BIT unit consisted of seven members with strong backgrounds in economics, psychology, randomized controlled trials, and/or government policymaking. As we documented in chapter 1, one of the first targets of Halpern and his colleagues was getting money out of people who weren't paying their taxes—consistent with Cameron's goal of saving money. This choice was brilliant. While some might argue that education, health, the environment, and so on are more important, a push to collect back taxes would have very few political opponents. In addition, collecting taxes provides a terrific proof of the nudge concept, even for the most skeptical politicians.

The goals of the nudge unit included making public services more cost-effective and easier to use and improving outcomes across government agencies by incorporating a more realistic model of human behavior. BIT has strived to meet these goals by understanding the context of a specific government ministry, considering what the existing literature might suggest as good alternatives, designing one or more interventions, and testing the interventions through randomized controlled trials. It was this testing that led the nudge unit to have a transformative effect on the use of experiments in governments throughout the world.

The direct accomplishments of the nudge unit are impressive. After the successful letter rewrite, the tax collection agency created its own nudge unit, as did numerous other government departments, and BIT worked on a range of initiatives: reducing the need for the government to repossess the property of hundreds of thousands of citizens who owed fines, increasing the number of organ donors available, improving energy efficiency, reducing medical prescription errors, encouraging charitable contribution in the London office of Deutsche Bank, increasing voting rates in British elections, improving employment rates at job centers, boosting insulation of homes, enhancing the diversity of the police force without lowering standards, reducing dropout rates in adult literacy classes, increasing minority enrollment in universities, improving road safety, and ensuring that British retirees choose the right pension program. Collectively, BIT has been effective in a wide range of policy areas, in helping to diffuse the nudge concept worldwide, and in highlighting the key role of experiments in behavioral policy implementation.

Facing increasing demand for its services in the UK and abroad, BIT was spun out of government in February 2014, to afford it the greater flexibility of being a social purpose company. It is owned by government, Nesta (a large innovation charity), and its own employees. Over the subsequent five years, BIT expanded its number of employees to over 150, its number of offices (now including London, Manchester, Singapore, New York, Wellington, and Sydney), and the diversity of firm activity. It also started to look less like a government office and more like a consulting firm—which it was.

Other countries, local and regional governments, and not-for-profits followed in BIT's footsteps. In 2015, President Obama set up the Social and Behavioral Science Initiative within the White House Office of Science and Technology to build on BIT's success. Other national governments with nudge units by 2017 included Australia, Canada, Mexico, Finland, Singapore, Italy, and India, with many other countries in the wings. BIT's New York office focused on cities, and Chicago and Rio de Janeiro created their own municipal initiatives. The European Commission, the Organisation for Economic Co-operation and Development, and the World Bank also created behavioral insight units. As of 2018, there are hundreds of nudge units. Many of them use experiments to help them understand how to best leverage behavioral insights for the social good and figure out what works in this rapidly evolving field.

Part II Experiments in the Tech Sector

4

From the Behavioral Insights Team to Booking.com

In the years since the Behavioural Insights Team (BIT) launched in 2010, behavioral policy experiments have proliferated, and there are now hundreds of groups dedicated to baking behavioral insights into policy. Behavioral economists in governments ranging from the United Kingdom to France to Singapore have improved the lives of their citizens by adopting an experimental mindset.

Looking at the broader landscape, however, the experimental revolution is still in its infancy. While the British government has run hundreds of behavioral trials, many other governments (including the US federal government) have embraced behavioral experiments—especially of the "nudge" variety—at a much slower pace. More broadly, there is scope for more governments to systematize the use of behavioral experiments, even as they continue to grow at an impressive pace. Policy experiments continue to spread outside the behavioral insights world as well, in areas ranging from healthcare to education.

Companies are similarly in the midst of the experimental revolution, though they've been dipping their toes into experiments for decades. In 1975–1976, for example, the Campbell Soup Company set out to understand the impact of its marketing efforts. In one experiment, the company increased its TV advertising spending for its condensed soups in Chicago, Milwaukee, Minneapolis, and St. Louis by 50% and found that these cities showed a 3.8% increase in sales relative to five control cities. The company decided this was not a large enough increase to be worth the extra ad spending. In another experiment, Campbell's rolled out a new semi-condensed, single-serving soup in Boston, Philadelphia, Atlanta, and Oklahoma City. After eight months, Soup for One was meeting sales goals and did not seem to be cutting into demand for Campbell's condensed soups in treatment markets relative to six control markets.[1] While methods have evolved since these early corporate experiments, they were a harbinger of broader adoption of the experimental method within corporations.

Retail catalogs were another early adopter of experimentation in the corporate world. In one set of experiments, marketing professors Eric Anderson and Duncan Simester worked with two retailers to experiment with price changes in their catalogs. The companies wanted to see whether prices ending in $9 (such as $29 or $39) would lead to higher purchases. To explore, the companies sent out different versions of their catalogs. In some catalogs, they changed prices listed at the beginning and end of the catalog to end in $9; in others, they left them unchanged. The researchers found that having prices that end in $9 seemed to increase sales. In another experiment, they found that simply adding the word "sale" could further increase sales. It might not be surprising that companies that sell products via catalogs, along with those that try to engage customers through direct mail, were early adopters of experiments: randomization and data tracking are relatively straightforward in these contexts, and companies are eager to nudge would-be customers to make purchases.

But perhaps no sector has embraced the experimental method more than the tech sector, where it is now a standard component of managerial decision making. If you think the 500-plus experiments that BIT has run to date are impressive, consider the fact that Google has run more than 10,000—in 2018 alone!

At first glance, government nudge units and private tech companies might seem like strange bedfellows as early embracers of experiments. After all, BIT's first client was HMRC, a government agency stocked with suit-wearing civil servants trying to make sure people pay their taxes. What would they have in common with a team of 23-year-old engineers at Facebook, where the daily attire is closer to a pair of flip-flops and an American Giant hoodie, paired with a mint mojito from Philz Coffee? Why did experiments take hold in these two dramatically different environments—one a staid and steady bureaucracy, the other a bastion of youthful creativity?

It turns out that both these contexts, while very different, push beyond barriers that have historically prevented experiments from taking broader hold in organizations. Behavioral economists draw on roots in psychology and experimental economics to establish their experimental approaches. Meanwhile, the tech sector is driven by a pragmatic interest in innovation and the use of data to get results. In both cases, there was a lightbulb moment: the acknowledgment that evidence trumps intuition, and that experiments are becoming easier to run.

The culture of experimentation in behavioral economics and in tech companies was facilitated in part by circumstances that dramatically reduced the cost of experimentation in both fields. For nudge units, BIT realized it didn't need to create an expensive new infrastructure in order to experiment—it could simply tweak existing processes, from tax letters to text messages. Tech companies came to a similar realization that small changes to a website could make a big difference and that they were already tracking enough data to start evaluating the results of experiments.

In part II of the book, we'll explore the landscape of experimentation in tech companies. Not only are tech companies at the vanguard in using experiments to make better business decisions, but their ability to circumvent common barriers to experimentation suggests ways that other organizations can adopt a culture of experimentation.

Five Key Barriers to Experimentation

To get a better sense of how the tech sector became a hotbed of experiments, it is helpful to consider several common barriers to experimentation that organizations can face.

Barrier 1: Not enough participants

Experimentalists need to think not only about the magnitude of the effect they study, but also about its precision. Even a seemingly large difference between two randomly assigned groups can be chalked up to noise if the experiment's sample size is too small. Making a strong inference from an experiment with too few participants is like seeing a coin flip yield two heads in a row and concluding that the coin must be unfair.

While many organizations can struggle to ensure a large enough sample, HMRC and tech companies like Google have access to enough participants to run many experiments. The government can draw on the full population of citizens, while Google can sample from its millions of users. The availability of large subject pools has contributed to these organizations being early adopters of experimental methods, as they were quick to realize the value of the large samples they had access to.

Many organizations now run experiments on a dramatically larger scale than academic researchers, both in the number and the scope of the experiments they run. At most university labs, there may be no more than a few hundred subjects available for lab experiments (about the same number of people who work in a mid-sized call center). In other words, for some types of experiments, a call center can experiment as easily as a university.

In practice, however, even tech companies sometimes struggle with sample size. We might assume, for example, that Uber has enough drivers to run as many experiments as it wants. But as we'll see in chapter 9, Uber runs some of its experiments at the market level, over a relatively small number of markets—to understand how changes affect the evolution of a market as a whole. New statistical approaches can help improve the inferences drawn from smaller experiments, which has also increased organizations' ability to experiment. As a result, the owner of a set of Jiffy Lube stores now has the potential to meaningfully run experiments as well.

Barrier 2: Randomization can be hard to implement

Without diligent randomization, it's hard to know whether a factor of interest is actually causing whatever an experiment seems to reveal. In the context of behavioral policy interventions, governments began to realize that their communications with citizens—including tax letters, text messages, and phone calls—were simple to randomize, making certain types of experiments easier and cheaper to run. While these units now run much more intensive experiments as well, they were quick to observe that communications were an easy touchpoint for their early forays into experimentation.

Online platforms such as Google, Facebook, and Amazon make it even easier to vary what individual customers see, thus simplifying the randomization process and implementation of experiments. The major tech platforms now all have an off-the-shelf approach to randomization that allows them to easily show some users one design of a webpage and other users a different one, and then track how user behavior differs across the different designs.

To see how the challenge of randomization has been mitigated, imagine if eBay were to advertise on a billboard on Route 66. There is virtually no way eBay could vary experimentally which Route 66 drivers saw the billboard and then track whether they make eBay purchases. In contrast, as we'll see in chapter 6, if eBay advertises on Google, it's fairly straightforward to randomize which users see the ads and to track whether they ultimately make purchases on eBay.

Barrier 3: Experiments require data to measure their impact

Lack of data has long been (and often continues to be) a major barrier to experimentation, since evaluating the effect of an experiment requires relevant outcome data to be measured—which can be costly and complicated. The digital age has led to an easier ability to track outcomes, at least for a subset of managerially relevant metrics.

To see both the promise and the peril of using online data to measure outcomes in an experiment, consider a newspaper that is testing different headlines for a story and using the number of people who click on the headline as a metric of success. The digital age and online reading have made it much easier to run headline experiments such as this, in part because the platform allows for new data to be analyzed (in this case, an indicator for whether or not someone clicks on the article). But while getting more readers is a good thing, it's far from the only thing a newspaper cares about. A newspaper would want readers not only to click on an article but to read it, be informed by it, and become (or remain) long-term readers of the paper. Hence, a clickbait headline might bring more readers in the short term, while also being completely disastrous in the longer term. As a result, successful experimenters need to think carefully about what data to use. More broadly, choosing the right outcome metrics remains a significant challenge even as measurement has gotten easier.

When designing an experiment with a company, we always start by doing a data audit to understand what data they are already collecting. We look at the outcomes they (and we) are interested in, and then see what data they have that might shed light on these outcomes and how to best create a map between the data they have and the ideal data set. We then explore external data as an investment to augment internal data.

To get a sense of how this might work, consider the following analysis from a major vacuum manufacturer. The company had been regularly tweaking its vacuums, exploring potential product improvements such as engineering redesigns aimed at increasing suction. To see whether the changes improved performance, the company adapted a series of tests Consumer Reports designed to evaluate vacuums. For example, in its vacuum ratings, Consumer Reports adapts "an industry-standard test to lift 10 grams of surface talc and 90 grams of embedded sand from a medium-pile carpet. The soiled carpet and vacuum are weighed to get a baseline measurement. Then, after a specific series of back-and-forth strokes across the test area performed in a climate-controlled chamber, the carpet and vacuum are weighed again to determine precisely how much debris was cleaned up."[2] The company created an internal lab in which it could run this exact test, which would tell it exactly how Consumer Reports would rate its vacuums.

The problem, however, was that no one is really trying to get 10 grams of surface talc and 90 grams of embedded sand from an otherwise glorious medium-pile carpet. (If you're like Mike, you're trying to get some combination of mac and cheese, hurled spinach, and squished blueberries out of a rug that was carefully chosen to allow these stains to blend in as part of the pattern.) While these tests surely said something about product quality—and were of direct interest, since many vacuum purchases look at Consumer Reports—the company was more broadly interested in building vacuums that consumers would find useful and keep buying over time.

In principle, the company knew it could run experiments to find out what features consumers liked, such as by offering one version of a vacuum in some markets and a different version in other markets. It tracked sales, which is of course extremely helpful. It also tracked returns, which helped to give a deeper (though still noisy) sense of whether people actually liked the vacuums they were buying.

With an eye toward the longer term, the company wanted to know about customer satisfaction. So it started collecting data on its Amazon reviews and using them not only to evaluate satisfaction but to continue to innovate its vacuums. The measure was another helpful addition, allowing the company to understand how people actually use its vacuums, what people like, what people don't like, and how the company could improve. For this company, online reviews facilitated experimentation by increasing data availability and making it easier to understand the effects of product changes.

Stepping back, there is almost never a perfect set of metrics. Setting the right set of outcomes requires a deep understanding of an organization's goals and the tradeoffs it is willing to make, as well as an understanding of what data is available and how the data that are observed ultimately map to the data the organization cares most about. Throughout part II, we'll explore this from the context of different tech companies and think about the ways in which they made decisions from experimental data.

Barrier 4: Underappreciation of decision makers' unpredictability

The original writers of the UK tax letter probably didn't think they wrote a bad letter, or, for that matter, the best possible one. As we mentioned in chapter 1, they probably thought it didn't much matter how the letter was written—a common assumption. As a consequence of this mindset, experimentation has historically been stifled.

All else being equal, an experiment is most valuable when you are least sure about which outcome is better. When people expect decision makers' behavior to be fairly stable and predictable, they will underestimate the value of experimentation.

Yet, as discussed in the last chapter, one of the great contributions of psychology has been an enhanced understanding of how fragile, context-specific, and sensitive to framing decision making can be. Psychologists have shaped this appreciation in government. In the tech sector, rapid iteration of products that seemed to yield rapidly different user behavior led companies to intuit what psychologists have long known: people sometimes make weird and unpredictable decisions. As we'll discuss, Google executives may all have guesses as to how people will react to different color backgrounds of the company's advertisements—but the truth is, it's hard to know.

To see why experiments came to be standard operating procedure in the tech sector, it's helpful to appreciate just how straightforward experiments in online platforms can be in some cases—at least relative to other contexts. In the simplest experiments (which, as we'll explain, still have challenges), a platform can simply show different versions of the same webpage to different sets of users and see which leads to the outcome they are interested in (e.g., more time on the platform, or more clicks on a certain feature). In cases where looking at short-term behavior on the platform is informative, the platform can experiment and adapt virtually in real time. And it is this rapid adaptation that allows companies to know that small changes can make a big difference.

Barrier 5: Overconfidence in our ability to guess the effect of an intervention

When making decisions, we often fail to appreciate just how wrong our intuition can be. Overconfidence can lead managers to go with their gut rather than to experiment to determine what the best course of action would be. Government nudge units came prepackaged with a keen understanding of the dangers of overconfidence. And in the tech sector, quick feedback from product launches, coupled with oodles of data, provide humbling reminders that we don't always know what will work. As we'll see, eBay presumably thought that its advertising strategy was just fine, until it ran an experiment that showed otherwise.

The Case of Google

Whenever managers are deciding whether to experiment, the five barriers to implementation that we've described can stand in the way. Fortunately, over time these barriers are melting away in many contexts. The tech sector and BIT units became early adopters of experiments because these barriers didn't pose much of a challenge for them and because they had so much to gain from simple, cheap experiments.

Suppose you were working on Google's advertising team and had to decide whether ads should have a blue background or a yellow background. Based on intuition, you might think that a blue background would better draw users' attention to the ad. Or you might prefer yellow, thinking it might leave users feeling happier and hence more interested in the ad. Suppose that, after having a designer play around with different colors, you decide that yellow feels like the right choice. You check in with your colleague, who decides, based on similar intuition and tinkering, that blue would lead to more successful searches. How would you decide which color to go with? In Google's early days, personnel might debate the issue until either someone caved, a manager decided for them, or a compromise was reached: "Fine, let's split the difference and go with green. Now, let's discuss what size font to use."

It quickly dawned on managers throughout Google that they didn't need to guess and debate; they could instead run an experiment to reach a more informed decision. Traditional barriers to experimentation melted away: Participants? They had billions. Randomization? Piece of cake. Data? They had that, too, as Google tracks every move you make on its platform. This left only two main barriers: first, realizing that the color of the background might actually matter, and second, having the humility needed to recognize that it's hard to know which is better. Once they got over those humps, experimentation became a no-brainer.

We recently chatted with Hal Varian, Google's chief economist, about the growing culture of experimentation at Google. "We don't want high-level executives discussing whether a blue background or a yellow background will lead to more ad clicks," he told us. "Why debate this point, since we can simply run an experiment to find out?"

Working with the group that developed Google's experimental infrastructure, Varian helped the company develop a systematic approach to experimentation—and an experimental mindset—precisely to avoid the sorts of barriers we've described. Google now runs experiments at an extraordinary scale—more than 10,000 per year, about half of them related to Google's advertising products and the other half related to its search engine. The assumption within the company is that the results of these experiments will inform managerial decisions in a variety of contexts. This mindset has permeated the tech sector more broadly. At the same time, even tech companies that are leading the charge on experiments still struggle with issues ranging from choosing the right outcomes to thinking about when and how long to run experiments.

Experimental Infrastructure at Booking.com

Like Google, the major tech companies, including Amazon, Facebook, Uber, Yelp, and TripAdvisor, all run thousands of experiments per year. Typically, they have a formal infrastructure that allows virtually every team to run experiments.

Consider the travel booking platform Booking.com. At Booking, a product manager can easily run an experiment to test any (and every) new product feature before rolling it out to all customers. Approximately 80% of Booking's product development teams are actively running experiments. Experiments are run in all parts of the business, from customer-facing platform experiments to partner-facing ones to customer service and marketing. That amounts to about 1,500 employees running experiments—many of whom have management or engineering backgrounds but limited prior knowledge of statistics or experimentation. To build a culture of experimentation, Booking implemented a variety of managerial changes, ranging from trainings run by in-house data scientists (including Lukas Vermeer, who gave us an overview of their current process) to more bespoke analytical support for individual experiments. Having an easy-to-use experimental infrastructure makes it relatively straightforward for the company to design and launch basic experiments.[3]

Once an experiment has run, the results are logged into a centralized repository that allows anyone on a team to peruse prior experiments, looking at what features were tested, regardless of whether a feature was ultimately implemented. A standard set of metrics are reported by default, but teams can customize the exact choice of metrics for the particular experiments they are running.

Experimental infrastructures like Booking's have two important practical implications. First, they allow companies to infuse most product-related decisions with experimental evidence. Ultimately, teams retain control over how to move from experimental results to a managerial decision. Teams have some flexibility regarding which metrics to analyze as outcomes and how much weight to give to each. Second, they help a larger set of employees to obtain a basic understanding of experimental methods, including the idea of hypothesis testing, practical significance (meaning the magnitude of effects), statistical significance, and the strengths and limitations of different outcome metrics.

Booking's setup is an increasingly common one within larger tech companies. Leading startups also run experiments, though often fewer of them and in a more bespoke matter. For example, Paktor—a Singapore-based dating app that Mike collaborates with—launches about one experiment every two weeks. And, increasingly, offline organizations—ranging from the Commonwealth Bank of Australia to Walmart—are exploring ways to experiment on a broader scale and in ways that can inform their most pressing decisions.

The Returns on Experimentation

Experiments have generated large returns for tech companies. To give just a few examples:

- Microsoft's search engine, Bing, ran an experiment in which it varied the physical size of ads on the screen. Bing found that increasing the size of advertisements increased user engagement, even though users saw fewer total ads. This simple change generated an additional $50 million per year in profits, according to Ron Kohavi, a VP of experimentation at Microsoft's Cloud and AI group.[4]

- Drawing on economic theory, economists Michael Ostrovsky and Michael Schwarz ran an experiment at Yahoo in which they tested new rules pertaining to the auction system it used to sell advertisements and increased Yahoo's profits by millions of dollars per year.[5]

- Amazon found that moving credit card offers from the homepage to the shopping cart page increased profits by millions of dollars.[6]

- As we'll see in chapter 8, StubHub ran an experiment that led the company to change the timing at which fees are presented to customers—a trivial change that led to a large boost in revenue.

Experiments have also led to decisions to cease expensive and ineffective programs (or, even better, to keep them from being implemented in the first place). For example, Microsoft spent $25 million to integrate content from Facebook and Twitter onto the Bing search page, only to have an experiment show that doing so led to trivial changes in engagement and revenue.[7] As we'll see in chapter 6, an experiment saved eBay $50 million per year in advertising spending.

Smart experiments can help to improve product design, shape advertising decisions, and guide investment. Yet experiments present challenges as well. In the following chapters, we'll describe notable experiments run by companies such as eBay, Uber, Facebook, Alibaba, and Upwork as we work toward principles for better understanding the value and limitations of experiments in the tech sector and beyond.

5
#AirbnbWhileBlack

"On the Internet, nobody knows you're a dog." That's the caption from a 1993 *New Yorker* cartoon by Peter Steiner, spoken by one dog seated at a computer to another dog. The cartoon spoke volumes about the perceived anonymity that had come to define large swaths of the early Internet. Perhaps nowhere was the ability to interact and transact anonymously more transformative than in the first generation of e-commerce platforms. Hypothetically speaking, an espresso drinker from Cambridge, Massachusetts could go online and buy a used Jura Impressa J9 espresso machine, sight unseen, from a stranger living in Berkeley, California. (If you've spent time in both towns, you would likely be unsurprised if these two cities were involved in such a transaction.)

In the Internet age, insurance got cheaper. Travel became easier to plan. A wider variety of books was sold. In each of these examples, the Internet allowed markets to become more efficient and left consumers better off. Things were looking good in the early days of online shopping.

Beyond these efficiency gains, there was another, subtler implication of the rise of e-commerce. By facilitating arm's-length transactions that obfuscated and deemphasized markers of race and gender

"On the Internet, nobody knows you're a dog."

Peter Steiner/The New Yorker Collection/The Cartoon Bank, © Condé Nast

from the buying process, the Internet created the potential to reduce the discrimination that had long plagued offline markets. Consider, for example, the case of car purchases, where discrimination has been documented for decades. Economists Fiona Scott Morton, Florian Zettelmeyer, and Jorge Silva-Risso found that car sales initiated online exhibited less of the racism and misogyny in price that persisted in transactions conducted offline and in person.[1] Markets were not only becoming more efficient—they were becoming fairer as well.

But this techno-utopian vision was not to last.

The *New Yorker* Updates Its Cartoon

Fast forward to 2011. Mike, a first-year faculty member at the time, was fascinated by online marketplaces, and suspected that even some of the seemingly innocuous design choices that newer platforms such as Airbnb, Uber, and Upwork were making had the potential to shape market outcomes. At that point, eBay and Amazon had been around for 15 years.

There was something different about Airbnb and the other second-generation platforms that were beginning to emerge. In contrast to the anonymity that marked some of the earlier e-commerce platforms, personal profiles, like the ones on Airbnb which included names and often pictures of renters and landlords, were an important part of these new platforms. In addition, hosts at that time were allowed to reject guests whenever they wanted to, without having to explain why. For a while, Airbnb would penalize hosts for rejecting guests—for example, by placing their properties lower in search results. But after one host's property was damaged in a high-profile incident, Airbnb removed the penalty and encouraged hosts to reject guests when they felt uncomfortable with them, even though hosts had little information about guests to go on. Over time, versions of the earlier penalty for rejecting guests have been reinstated, and Airbnb has used experiments to evaluate options around penalizing hosts for rejecting guests.

Compare this situation to the travel site Expedia, where property managers (primarily of hotels) simply list room availability, and virtually anyone can book with a credit card. Clearly, Airbnb was bringing dramatic changes to the market. Rather than being a widespread feature of the Internet (as suggested by the 1993 *New Yorker* cartoon), anonymity was becoming a design choice that platforms could make or not make.

With his colleague Ben Edelman, Mike wrote a case study about Airbnb with the goal of understanding the platform's approach to building trust and getting people to feel comfortable allowing strangers into the intimacy of their homes. Initially, we were thinking about the general problem of building trust (this was before we had begun the empirical research on discrimination). Through this process, we noticed how prominent personal profiles were on the platform, coupled with the flexibility the site gave hosts to reject users—and we wondered whether this would raise the potential for discrimination that would be difficult to engage in in other marketplaces. Would hosts be unwilling to rent to people of other races and ethnicities? Starting with the landmark Fair Housing Act of 1968, the US government had spent half a century battling discrimination in offline rental markets. Through regulation and enforcement, the efforts had succeeded in reducing rates of discrimination, both in hotels and long-term rentals. Airbnb now raised the prospect of erasing these hard-won gains. We shared the case study with Airbnb, and Mike spoke with people who worked at the company. Perhaps unsurprisingly, Airbnb wasn't interested in this new line of investigation. The company repeatedly, and publicly, denied that any bias was occurring on its platform.

The idea of anonymous arm's-length transactions continued to fade from new e-commerce platforms, and with it, the promise of a more equitable Internet age. In 2015, the *New Yorker* published an updated cartoon, this one by Kamraan Hafeez, featuring the anonymous dogs from the 1993 cartoon. The caption? "Remember when, on the Internet, nobody knew who you were?"

"Remember when, on the Internet, nobody knew who you were?"

Kaamran Hafeez/The New Yorker Collection/The Cartoon Bank, © Condé Nast

Airbnb's Moral Wiggle Room

In 2014, Reed Kennedy, a successful tech entrepreneur and investor, found himself being repeatedly rejected on Airbnb. Reed is black, and he suspected that discrimination played a role. His profile includes a photo of himself, so race is likely the first thing hosts see when deciding whether or not he is worthy of staying in their rental properties. Reed reached out to the company with his suspicions about the rejections, thinking they would want to know.

He received an email from a company representative in reply: "I can assure you that the incidents where you've been declined by hosts has absolutely nothing to do with your race or ethnicity." The message continued, "You've been doing a great job reaching out to multiple hosts to find the best place suitable for you. I appreciate your concern and I want you to know that Airbnb takes discrimination seriously. If there was any cause for concern, we would have reached out to the hosts immediately. However, hosts have the freedom to decline requests for any reason." Well, which one is it? Are hosts not allowed to discriminate? Or are they allowed to reject guests for any reason?

The representative went on to tell Reed how he could increase his chances of getting a room. First, the person suggested he should get references to vouch for him. "References are a great way for your friends to vouch for (and brag about!) you. They help you build a trustworthy reputation in the Airbnb community since they appear right on your public profile. You can request references via email, Facebook, or Airbnb by going to your Profile > References > Request References. A reference will only display in your public profile if the person who wrote it has a profile picture on their Airbnb account." Ok, fine. So, Reed should get some references—but those references needed to have pictures on Airbnb, too. But what if the references were also ... oh, never mind.

Second, the Airbnb rep suggested Reed look for a place that would take anyone and forget about places where he would actually *prefer* to stay. "I would suggest using our Instant Book feature," she wrote. "If a listing has Instant Book turned on, you can book it without having to wait for the host's confirmation." Lucky Reed. He could stay anywhere he liked, as long as the host wasn't discriminatory.

The representative went on to tell Reed that he'd be OK if he just listened to her suggestions. At the same time, she acknowledged that the listings he had contacted were, in fact, still available. She even encouraged him to "reach back out to the hosts once you've had a few references created on your behalf." In the end, the representative offered Reed a $100 voucher for his troubles. But the real coup de grace came in the closing of the email: "I wish you lots of success with booking reservations through Airbnb, Reed. I can tell by your picture that you're a nice guy."[2]

By this time, Mike had already worked with Ben on the case study of Airbnb, as well as a 2014 analysis of data we had plucked from the Airbnb platform that was suggestive—but not definitive—of discrimination against hosts by guests.[3] The paper showed, among other findings, that African American hosts were earning less money per night on the platform than white hosts with similar listings. It seemed not much of a leap to expect that there might also be discrimination against African American guests by hosts.

Mike and Ben then added Dan Svirsky, an economics PhD student who also held a law degree, to the team to continue exploring the issue. We set out to run an experiment to answer the question at hand: Was discrimination against guests a real problem on Airbnb?

When he read in the news that Mike was conducting research on Airbnb, Reed got in touch with Mike and told him what had happened to him. As you may have guessed by now, Mike found Airbnb's response to Reed to be unsatisfying. How could Airbnb be so sure that Reed wasn't being discriminated against? Of course, the company couldn't, not without gathering data—which they seemed uninterested in. The response of this customer service representative was consistent with the broader strategy the company seemed to be taking: exploiting its moral wiggle room, strategically choosing to avoid looking for evidence of discrimination in order to avoid having to do anything about it.

The central factor that allowed Airbnb executives to be so nonchalant was the ambiguity of the nonexperimental evidence at hand, which was suggestive but not definitive. If they knew for certain that discrimination was a widespread problem on the platform, they might feel compelled—whether by regulation, public pressure, or human decency—to proactively address the issue. But as long as Airbnb executives could contort the evidence to convince themselves and others that discrimination wasn't a problem, they could continue to write it off as a nonissue.

Airbnb continued its repeated denials and what seemed like head-in-the-sand tactics. After Mike and Ben's 2014 paper (but before our experiment), the company put out a press release dodging the issue and disregarding the data surrounding it. (Stories like Reed's continued to come out of the woodwork, but Airbnb seemed to have no intention of trying to understand, let alone tackle, the issue.)

At the time that Reed was exchanging emails with Airbnb's customer service department, Mike was running his experiment with Ben and Dan. Posing as guests, we sent rental inquiries to some 6,400 Airbnb hosts in the United States. All the inquiries were identical, except for one trait: half were from (fictitious) guests with names that are more common among white people, as determined by birth records (such as Brett and Todd), while the rest were from guests with names that are more common among black people (specifically, names that were statistically more common among African Americans, such as Darnell and Jamal). In other words, we chose names that would signal the guest's race. For this research, we did not include photos (the reason being that adding photos would make it harder for us to say that the profiles were truly identical other than race). This was similar to the approach that economists Marianne Bertrand and Sendhil Mullainathan had used to understand discrimination in labor markets in 2001 and 2002, and evocative of work that governments had done in assessing discrimination in offline housing markets, dating back to at least the 1970s.[4]

The results were, in a word, depressing. Inquiries from guests with distinctively African American sounding names were 16% less likely to get a yes from the hosts than those with white-sounding names. We found discrimination across a range of neighborhoods and listing types, from inexpensive to costly, from separate apartments to guest rooms, and from small-time landlords to larger ones who were breaking the law by violating the Fair Housing Act.

When we've talked about these results, we are occasionally asked whether hosts are more likely to reject African Americans because they believe that African Americans are simply worse guests in general than people of other races (economists refer to this as statistical discrimination, since the hosts are using race to statistically infer something else about the guest). Our data provides insight into this question: the discrimination we observed is concentrated among hosts who have never even had a black guest (based on previous reviews) and thus had no experience on which to base their prejudice. By contrast, those who did have experience with black guests were far less likely to discriminate against them in our experiment. Thus, any inferences that black applicants are systematically different than white applicants must be coming from general stereotypes, and explicit or implicit racism, rather than from prior experience with black guests. This also highlights that one potential channel for reducing bias—exposure to people from other groups—is unlikely to eliminate the bias we observe on Airbnb.

#AirbnbWhileBlack

The results of our study became public in December 2015. Combined with a groundswell of frustration from users who had been discriminated against on the platform, this created pressure from Airbnb users, journalists, and government officials. No longer could Airbnb hide behind its unfounded assertions that discrimination was not an issue on the platform. As public pressure on the company mounted, Ben and Mike received an email from a former colleague who was by then a senior leader at Airbnb. The friend flew to Boston and came to Mike's house for pizza. The details of the conversation were off the record, but the friend seemed optimistic that he could convince the company to do something about the racial discrimination we'd identified.

At the same time, government lawyers and policymakers began weighing Airbnb's culpability in the matter. Some users began to wonder whether they really wanted to support a company like Airbnb. The NPR show *Hidden Brain* aired an episode on our findings, then hosted a Twitter chat in which hundreds of people shared their stories of discrimination on Airbnb using the hashtag #AirbnbWhileBlack. The Congressional Black Caucus wrote to the CEO of Airbnb, urging the company to take action:

> Will Airbnb consider implementing some common sense measures to avoid discrimination of their customers like those suggested by Dr. Michael Luca in the June 2, 2016, Washington Post article which suggested fixes such as "downplaying when and where Airbnb displays guests" pictures and names; increasing the use of the instant booking feature that eliminates the subjective dialogue with hosts deciding which reservations to book; and converting Airbnb's anti-discrimination policy into regular notices each time someone books a reservation.

Our experiment and proposed solutions helped to facilitate an evidence-based conversation, and the company ultimately decided to take action based on our findings. Airbnb hired a task force made up of high-profile civil rights activists. The task force included former attorney general Eric Holder; Laura Murphy, the director of the ACLU's legislative office; and a number of academics. Of course, this effort was at least partially motivated by the desire to defuse a PR crisis that was damaging the company's reputation and possibly its bottom line. From a business perspective, it was clear that Airbnb's design choices had facilitated discrimination and that the company was well positioned to make changes. Now it was up to Airbnb to deliver.

Airbnb Makes Design Changes

Airbnb's task force could have chosen to advocate for one of three broad directions.

At one extreme, Airbnb could continue with the status quo and do nothing to reduce discrimination. At the other extreme, the company could completely eliminate names, pictures, and all other identifying information from user profiles. This option would be sure to purge the platform of most of the discrimination it was facing, but it also imposed risks. Personal profiles offered a cheap tool for building superficial trust between Airbnb users. Taking them away could sacrifice some of that trust.

The third option would be to keep users' names and pictures in their profiles, but to implement other changes in the hopes of reducing discrimination. These changes could include making pictures less salient (for example, by making them smaller or putting them in a less prominent location), getting more hosts to adopt Instant Book (which allowed guests to sign up for available dates on the spot), or updating the terms and conditions to more explicitly prohibit discrimination—ideas we had proposed in conversations, and also in a *Harvard Business Review* article.[5]

Take a minute to imagine that you're a member of Airbnb's task force. What would you propose? What target (if any) would you set for reducing discrimination? How would you measure success?

The task force's proposal arrived in September 2016,[6] five years after our research team initially contacted Airbnb, two years after our first paper documenting suggestive evidence of discrimination, and nearly a year after the experiment had gone public and we had made an initial set of recommendations.

The company decided to take the middle road. Hosts could continue to view a guest's name and picture, and then decide whether to reject the guest. But the company also committed to nibbling around the edges to try to reduce discrimination. The proposals ranged from optional bias training for hosts (though they don't report how many have taken it) to helping guests who were denied a booking on the basis of race in finding alternative accommodations. The most promising proposal was a commitment to increase the number of hosts who would accept qualified guests without looking at their profile information beforehand (via the Instant Book feature that had been recommended to Reed). In its report, the company committed to "making one million listings bookable via Instant Book by January 2017." Airbnb also thought about discrimination against hosts. To this end, the company followed Mike's suggestion of removing the pictures of hosts from the main search results page, which meant that guests needed to click one page down to see a host's picture. At the time, guest pictures remained very salient on the platform.

Satisfied with the Changes?

Following Mike's experiment, Airbnb created a data science team to study the issue and to explore potential solutions. For example, they committed to "experiment with reducing the prominence of guest photos in the booking process." In short, Airbnb would run experiments to test the effects of possible changes designed to reduce discrimination.

To give a sense of the types of experiments they were running, consider their goal of increasing the proportion of listings that would be available through instant booking. There are many ways to accomplish this. They could change the default option for hosts to "instant booking," asking them to proactively change their setting if they wanted to opt out of it (much as in the default discussion we had in chapter 3). Alternatively, they could pay hosts to sign up for instant booking. Or they could prioritize listings that are available for instant booking, and allow market forces to reward hosts to sign up. Airbnb ran experiments testing a variety of options such as these.

When testing potential changes, Airbnb would essentially ask, Would such a move make hosts less discriminatory? The company also considered a second question: Would these changes cost the company money, or lead to a worse experience (for hosts and/or guests)? When they had the answers, they determined what changes to implement by making tradeoffs on how much discrimination they were willing to retain on the platform to avoid alienating users (some of whom may have liked having the option to discriminate).

To be clear, we love the fact that Airbnb was running experiments to answer such tricky questions. But we also found it disappointing that Airbnb hid the results of its experiments, hid the tradeoffs it was making even though they were relevant to policymakers and users, and hid the overall impact of its changes—from policymakers and from the general public. When a company maintains such secrecy, it's hard not to assume that no news is bad news—in this case, that plenty of discrimination will continue to occur. Transparency would be an important next step for Airbnb.

Regulators also continued to take notice. In the spring of 2017, Airbnb and the state of California reached a deal that will allow the state to conduct tests for discrimination on the platform—small-scale versions of the experiment we had run. This will allow the state to identify discrimination on an ongoing basis and step up enforcement where necessary.

The company's design has also continued to evolve, and in 2018 Airbnb announced that hosts would not be able to see the pictures of guests until after the host decided whether or not to accept the guest. From our discussions with employees at the company, it's clear that there are people working there who are deeply dedicated to reducing bias. It's also clear that a lot needs to be done to create a more equitable tech sector.

The Broader Value of Experiments

Experiments have played a pivotal role throughout Airbnb's discrimination struggles. It was an experiment that first brought the problem to light and forced Airbnb to confront the issue. It was a series of experiments that allowed Airbnb to understand how different design choices would affect the level of discrimination that was occurring and ultimately shape the changes it made. And experiments will ultimately allow regulators to identify and regulate discrimination on the platform.

While we hate that discrimination exists on Airbnb, we are happy that experiments have helped to identify and reduce the problem. More broadly, the Airbnb saga highlights the ability of experiments to illuminate and improve the world around us. Companies and governments need a better sense of the value and risks of experiments, as well as how to implement them. Policymakers, companies, and researchers need to have more conversation through experiments, replacing intuition and emotion with solid evidence.

In particular, experiments can benefit organizations in four main ways, as we will see throughout the book:

Purpose 1: Testing theory and mechanisms

As we've mentioned, one potential hypothesis (though not ours) in Mike, Ben, and Dan's Airbnb experiment might have been that hosts were discriminating against African Americans because they had had bad experiences with African American guests. By combining experimental results with data about Airbnb hosts' prior guests, we were able to test that theory and show that this was not, in fact, what was happening.

More generally, in many situations, managers have a theory about what is happening in a certain situation. Running an experiment can help to confirm (or disconfirm) such theories and shed light on what social scientists refer to as mechanisms—in other words, what is driving the patterns we observe.

Purpose 2: Understanding magnitudes and tradeoffs

Our initial Airbnb experiment showed that African American guests were roughly 16% more likely to be rejected by hosts than white guests who were otherwise identical. It showed that discrimination was widespread—from hosts renting out a spare bedroom to landlords of large, expensive properties.

After Airbnb made the changes described above, what level of discrimination do you think remained on the platform? A 5% gap? 10%? Unfortunately, we just don't know, since Airbnb hasn't made the data public. Therefore, it's impossible to know what tradeoffs Airbnb accepted when making changes. For example, Airbnb might be OK with African Americans being 10% more likely to be rejected, if this meant that hosts would be 0.1% more likely to make a transaction overall. Transparent discussions of such tradeoffs would facilitate Airbnb's ongoing dialogue with regulators, employees, and users.

Experiments help clearly define the tradeoffs that are occurring as a result of design changes. Once they have identified these tradeoffs, they can be assured that if they disagree about a path forward, it's based on differences in tradeoff preferences rather than different guesses about what will work.

Purpose 3: Evaluating policies

Airbnb made a bunch of decisions about what bundle of changes to make. Get rid of host pictures from search page? Check. Get rid of host pictures from listing page? Nope. Take steps to increase instant booking? Yes. Require instant booking? No.

At the end of all of this, the company rolled out its redesigned platform. Because these changes affect one another, and because the company's experiments may have tested different options than the final version, there was value not only in testing individual theories, mechanisms, and tweaks, but also in evaluating the new page as a whole. This wouldn't allow Airbnb to identify exactly which tweaks were driving different levels of change, as earlier experiments had, but it would show the company the overall impact of its suite of changes.

Purpose 4: Fact finding

Sometimes you don't have a theory. Stepping away from the Airbnb example, there are plenty of times when you just want to make sure you're not breaking anything or missing some great innovation, or you just want to know what would happen if you tweaked a process. And that's a fine use of experiments, as we'll see in this part of the book as well—searching out facts where you think process might matter but don't know exactly how. For example, suppose you were helping eBay to choose its font. Should they switch to Courier? It may be hard to have a good theory for this. But it's easy just to check the results.

6

eBay's $50 Million Advertising Mistake

Have you ever wondered how Google makes money? After all, it doesn't charge us to search on its platform. To understand Google's business model, it's helpful to have a sense of how the platform operates. Google is known for being a powerful search engine that provides searchers with a list of links to other sites. To do so, Google begins by scouring the web and keeping tabs on the millions of websites Google users might find of interest—everything from travel companies to newspaper to retailers. The company invests heavily in an algorithm that analyzes results from past searches (yours and everyone else's) and tries to figure out which websites are most useful for any given search term. The output of that whole process is the set of links you are shown when you do a search. A search for "cheeseburger recipe" might link to various cooking websites.

Even though you don't pay for your Google searches, they are profitable for the company, because Google sells advertisements that appear alongside your search results. To see how this works, try a few Google searches. You'll see the links that are your main results—these are called the organic results. But above that, at least for some searches, you'll see a link with two letters next to it: "ad." These ads are how Google earns revenue from its search engine.

You may think of Google as a search engine, but businesses think of it as an advertising platform. Businesses can bid on search terms in an elaborate advertising auction that determines which ads will be shown to searchers. And it turns out that this is a very profitable business. In 2017 alone, the company made roughly $100 billion in advertising revenues.

While selling ads is lucrative for Google, it's unclear whether buying ads on Google is a good deal for the businesses that advertise on the platform. Take a look at the figure below, which shows the results from a Google search for clothing retailer the Gap. Notice that each of the first two links point back to the Gap's website—the first organic result and an ad above it. It makes sense that the first organic link is to the Gap's website. After all, if someone is Googling the Gap, they are probably looking for a link to, well, the Gap. Gap's decision to advertise on its brand name also seems reasonable. Gap executives may think this will help ensure that their company will be shown first in searches for its name, signal how much it believes in its brand, or make it harder for competitors (say, J. Crew or Uniqlo) to use advertisements to peel off customers searching for the Gap. Yet the actual impact of such ads is far from certain.

More than a century ago, department store magnate John Wanamaker quipped, "Half the money I spend on advertising is wasted; the trouble is, I don't know which half." The Internet age has offered renewed opportunity for organizations to estimate the effect of advertising, by conducting experiments.

Why Correlations are Misleading: Evidence from eBay

Like the Gap, eBay is already a pretty well-known company—and when you Google "eBay," "eBay shoes," etc., it's not surprising that the top result will be a link to an eBay page. So, when Steve Tadelis, a leading tech economist at UC Berkeley who at the time headed the gap   🔍

🔍 All   🗺 Maps   📰 News   🔗 Shopping   🖼 Images   ⋮ More   Settings   Tools

About 877,000,000 results (1.04 seconds)

Gap® Official Site | See What's New at Gap
[Ad] www.gap.com/ ▼
Meet In The **Gap**® - Shop This Season's Must-Have Essentials Picked Just for You. Denim For All. Free
Shipping On $50+ Explore The Swim Shop. Up To 50% Off Everything. Shop New Summer Arrivals.
50% Off Tees & Dresses. Free Returns On All Items.

Perfect Summer Outfits   Explore New Dress Styles
Find The Latest Summer-Ready Looks.   New Silhouettes Including Wrap,
Shop Shorts, Swim, Dresses, & More.   Cami Midi, And Button Down Shirt.

Shop Gap for Casual Women's, Men's, Maternity, Baby & Kids Clothes
https://www.gap.com/ ▼
Shop casual women's, men's, maternity, kids' & baby clothes at **Gap**. Our style is clean and confident,
comfortable and accessible, classic and modern. Find the ...

eBay's economics group, noticed that the company was also paying to advertise on Google when users searched for "eBay" and other brand-related keywords, he began to wonder whether they should switch their advertising strategy. Checking in with eBay's marketing team, Tadelis discovered that the company had been spending roughly $50 million per year on Google ads. The marketing group told him they thought it was a good investment, noting that many users who clicked on the ads ended up buying stuff on eBay. Wasn't that a win?

Steve was unconvinced. He pointed to the potential for selection bias: the ads were targeted; they were being shown to people who Googled the company and thus were already prepared to shop on eBay. In other words, there was a good chance these people would get to eBay even without the ads.

An experiment was in order. After all, why guess when eBay could replace intuition with causal evidence?

The eBay Ads Experiment

Working within eBay's economics research team, economists Tom Blake, Chris Nosko, and Steve Tadelis ran a series of experiments, seeking to find out exactly what the financial returns on Google ads were. They turned Google ads on and off, experimentally varying across markets. They tracked the traffic coming to eBay from Google ads. And, critically, they also tracked traffic coming from organic links—that is, from people who were going to eBay from unpaid Google search links.

The findings were stark. Naturally, eBay lost all of the traffic it had been getting from ads in the markets where it had turned off Google advertisements. However, eBay saw a spike in organic traffic—traffic from the unpaid Google search results—in these markets. What happened? Evidently, users who Googled "eBay" (or another eBay-related search term), who had been clicking on the ad because they saw no reason to scroll down to the organic link just below it, were now instead clicking on the first organic search result. For these searchers, eBay essentially swapped in free organic clicks for each advertising click lost. In other words, much of the money eBay was shelling out to Google each year was a waste. The company did find, however, that advertising for items that are less commonly associated with eBay could lead to a genuine boost in sales. For example, eBay benefits considerably more from advertising on the term "used gibson les paul," since searchers may not be thinking about eBay when searching for a guitar. What's more, ads were more effective for users who were not experienced eBay buyers, most likely because these users were less familiar with the variety of products that eBay offers. This finding supports the theory that ads are more effective when they provide information to less-informed potential customers.

Following the experiment, eBay cut back on its Google advertising campaign. A Google search for the term "eBay" now yields only the organic results, as eBay no longer advertises on the search term "eBay."

ebay   🔍

🔍 All   ⊘ Shopping   📕 Books   📰 News   🖾 Images   ⋮ More   Settings   Tools

About 2,150,000,000 results (0.72 seconds)

eBay: Electronics, Cars, Fashion, Collectibles, Coupons and More
https://www.ebay.com/ ▾
Buy and sell electronics, cars, fashion apparel, collectibles, sporting goods, digital cameras, baby items,
coupons, and everything else on **eBay**, the world's ...

Search ebay.com   🔍

eBay Motors   Daily Deals
eBay Motors makes it easy to find   We update our deals daily, so check
parts for cars, trucks, SUVs ...   back for the best deals ...

Electronics   All Categories
Get the best deal for Electronics from   All Categories on eBay - Shop,
the largest online selection ...   Explore and Discover from a ...

eBay's wasted ad spending highlights the danger of relying on correlations in decision making—in this case, between ad clicks and purchases—without thinking about why the correlation might not be causal. eBay's advertising experiment called into question its strategy for paying for search advertising. More broadly, it shows the importance of using experiments to find answers to important business questions.

After eBay's experiment went public, about 11% of large companies that did not face competitors' ads on their keywords (matching eBay's situation) ended up discontinuing their keyword advertising, according to research by Justin Rao and Andrey Simonov. However, the research also suggests that firms did not seem to learn the other important lesson—which is that they should have run their own advertising experiments.

The Return to Yelp Ads

The eBay experiment estimated the returns to ads for one large, well-branded company. One of us (Mike) and collaborators Daisy Dai and Hyunjin Kim set out to understand whether search advertising might be more effective for smaller businesses in a context where people were doing targeted searches. We reached out to Geoff Donaker, who was the COO of Yelp, a platform where people post reviews of local businesses and services. Yelp also sells ads to these businesses and services.

Cooperating with our large-scale experiment, Yelp gave thousands of restaurants free ads for three months. They gave the standard restaurant advertising packages that Yelp was selling at the time, which would provide at least 1,000 impressions of a restaurant's advertisement per month on the website. Ads would come up at various times—for example, searching for pizza might lead to an advertisement for T Anthony's pizzeria. Like eBay's advertising on Google, this was a form of search advertising. However, unlike advertising on Google, businesses did not choose their own keywords. Instead, Yelp used an algorithm to help figure out where and when to show the ads.

In contrast with the results of eBay's experiments, we found that advertising had a large effect for the small businesses in our sample. Businesses that were given advertisements saw spikes in visits to their pages, as well as in the metrics Yelp uses to measure consumer intention—such as calls to a restaurant, or searches for directions to a business.

These results reflect important differences between the two sets of experiments. eBay is a large brand with few competitors and broad awareness. In contrast, small businesses that advertise on Yelp tend to be less known and more likely to benefit from the brand awareness that an advertisement brings. Consistent with these observations, we found that Yelp ads were more impactful for independent businesses than for big chains (think McDonalds or Applebee's) that already have an established reputation. In addition, Yelp ads were more effective for higher-rated businesses. The ads were able to raise awareness of businesses, a result that is more valuable for higher-quality businesses. An ad for a high-quality restaurant may help to bring in repeat customers who are now aware of the restaurant and excited to keep going back.[1]

As you can see, organizations may reach very different results—and conclusions—from similar experiments. To understand the magnitude (or often even the direction) of an effect in particular contexts of interest, such as returns on advertising or the value of bonuses, organizations need to run experiments in a variety of contexts and to focus on developing frameworks, rather than simply relying on a single data point that they see from an experiment.

For example, marketing teams might want to run experiments to figure out the types of quirky keywords that seem to work for their brand, or the extent to which ads seem to have a longer brand effect for them, or the extent to which customers drawn in from advertisements are likely to become repeat customers. This is likely to vary across brands, across time, and across platforms. Although there is still a long way to go, the field of advertising is becoming more scientific, and even simple experiments have generated powerful insights.

7

Deep Discounts at Alibaba

As you might guess by now, we're pleased when we hear about organizations running experiments with the goal of improving their performance. But while experimentation is often a smart business decision, it's also true that not just any experiment will do. This chapter describes an experiment motivated by an important managerial goal—the experiment yields interesting results, but also highlights the managerial judgment involved in moving from experimental results to product decisions.

Chinese e-commerce giant Alibaba is the world's largest retailer, valued at more than $500 billion. Like Amazon, Alibaba is an online marketplace that allows other retailers to sell products on its platform. In 2016, the business was rapidly expanding, having experienced two straight years of quarterly revenue growth of greater than 50%. The company was constantly exploring ways to continue this remarkable growth, in part by running experiments aimed at improving its e-commerce business.

One area where Alibaba experimented involved the discounts it offered to users. While retailers were allowed to set their own prices on the platform, Alibaba maintained some control over the prices users ultimately paid, in part by determining when sellers could and couldn't offer customers targeted coupons. Alibaba wanted to identify the situations in which discounts would be most valuable for the platform, in terms of user engagement and retention.

Like most tech companies, Alibaba collected enormous amounts of user data, including information on each customer's browsing history, past purchases, and mobile location. The platform used its treasure trove of data to inform how it should target coupons. For example, customers would at times put items in their shopping cart without immediately purchasing them. They could return to their cart if they decided to purchase the item later, but many ended up not purchasing the products at all. To try to convert shopping cart items into purchases, Alibaba allowed sellers to offer deep discounts to customers who had left certain "promoted products" in their shopping cart for over 24 hours. Targeting a customer's shopping cart was potentially appealing because the coupon would only appear for products that the customer was on the fence about and might help to change their decision, as opposed to customers who would buy the product even without a discount. This strategy also had the advantage of reaching customers when purchasing decisions are top of mind (as opposed to, say, emailing a discount with an expiration date).

Did the program actually change customer behavior? In early 2016, a team of management researchers—Hengchen Dai, Lingxiu Dong, and Dennis Zhang—partnered with a team at Alibaba to conduct a randomized field experiment on two Alibaba platforms that would measure the precise impact of the shopping cart promotion program.

The researchers randomly selected one million Alibaba customers who had been targeted by at least one promotion on the platform between March 12, 2016 and April 11, 2016, and assigned them either to the control condition or the treatment condition. Customers in the treatment condition were shown coupons for certain promoted products that they had left in their shopping cart for more than a day. The control group, meanwhile, received no promotions at all.

Alibaba and the research team had to make some managerial decisions when designing the experiment, namely what outcomes to focus on and what factors to consider when deciding whether to continue, or even expand, the shopping cart promotion program. The team decided to look at (1) whether users were more likely to purchase the items in their carts when they were discounted, and (2) whether they bought more stuff overall from Alibaba.

Perhaps unsurprisingly, the results showed that users were more likely to buy a product if it was discounted in the shopping cart than if it was not discounted. However, they did not seem to be spending more money overall on Alibaba in the longer term (the researchers looked at data through at least a month after the coupon expired), suggesting either that the effect of the discount was small (relative to total spending) or that users were shifting purchases away from undiscounted products to discounted ones. These results suggested that the shopping cart program was a bit of a wash: good for some sellers, bad for others, and not market-expanding.

The team then looked a bit further, analyzing purchasing in the weeks after the treatment period, from April 12 to May 9, 2016. During this period, they found a modest uptick in engagement with the platform after the initial coupon was offered. For example, users who were offered a coupon looked at more things on the platform. So that's a good thing, if not terribly important. But there's a catch to this upside: customers who received a discount started adding more items to their shopping carts and letting them sit there, presumably in hope of triggering further discounts. In the long term, this pattern could be bad if it leads users to hold out for discounts instead of paying the list price of the items they want.[1]

From Data to Decisions

Should Alibaba continue the discount program? The answer depends in part on whose perspective we take. Sellers offering targeted discounts should be happy to see the discounts increase revenue (if not always profit). From their perspective, it is probably better to continue the program (though sellers might benefit from a no-discount regime, if it reduces competition).

Things are considerably murkier when we take the perspective of the platform. After all, the promotion doesn't seem to increase overall spending; it changes the way the pie is split rather than increasing the size of the pie. The longer-term implications of the experiment are also unclear. As in many tech experiments, Alibaba measured short-term effects of an intervention, but it cares about long-term value. If customers' strategic behavior (putting items in a cart and waiting for a discount) were to increase as awareness of the discount spread, the strategic behavior might undermine the intended targeting and cannibalize full-price sales.

Based on this experiment and internal discussions, Alibaba decided not to expand its shopping cart discount program. It's great that Alibaba was experimenting (and that the experiment was well implemented), but there's an important limitation to the map from results to the managerial decision—which is that Alibaba seemed to be asking an incomplete question. Alibaba's experiment essentially asked, "Should this program exist?" rather than "How should this program be designed?" This is an important distinction, since the shopping cart discount may have seen small effects simply because it was poorly designed rather than because such discounts are inherently flawed.

Specifically, there are several design elements of the shopping cart program that Alibaba might have thought more about. First, the promotion suffered from relatively low exposure—one-third of users did not revisit their shopping carts before the coupon expired (coupons expired on the day they were given), so they never knew the discount was being offered. This low-key placement of the discount (users weren't sent emails letting them know about it) meant that the discount program could have been easily overlooked. Alibaba could have varied exposure by doing more to raise awareness of the discounts, which might have dramatically changed users' behavior.

Second, the current program allowed sellers to choose the size of the discount they offered. This prohibited the experimenters from understanding the causal effect of discount size on purchase behavior. In their summary of the results, the authors of the experiment note that the "shopping-cart promotion program did not often give out large discounts (the average and median discount rates were 17% and 13%, respectively)." The program might have been more effective if Alibaba had used some of its available data to help make better recommendations about how much of a discount to offer.

Third, the impact of the discount program on user satisfaction and long-term engagement with Alibaba remains unclear. The research team is transparent about this, noting that their "experiment was not designed to focus on detecting the long-term effects of the promotion program." (The authors do find that users in the treatment condition search for more products in the following months, though this effect goes away within a year.) Even though this particular program was not very effective at changing overall engagement, a well-designed, well-implemented shopping cart discount program might still yield large returns for Alibaba.

Stepping back, this experiment highlights both the promise and the challenges of using experiments to guide managerial decisions. This experiment allowed Alibaba to replace intuition with data for a particular program it had already implemented, which marks an important step in the right direction. But it also left gaps in Alibaba's mental model of how to proceed. In addition to evaluating the existing promotion, Alibaba might learn more by testing different elements of it to better understand the mechanisms that make experiments more or less effective. As mentioned in chapter 2, Stanford economist and Nobel laureate Al Roth often refers to what he has learned from "a series of experiments" rather than from one particular experiment, because so much more insight can be gleaned from looking at sets of tests that tease out various mechanisms. While we applaud Alibaba for basing decisions on data (and the researchers for conducting a very cool experiment), the platform might benefit from running more experiments aimed at testing and refining its discounting program and other elements of its pricing strategy.

Ultimately, running successful experiments in organizations is as much about asking the right questions as it is about answering them. Managers should focus not only on testing a product as is, but on using experiments to develop frameworks that will help them make decisions. This means teasing out boundary conditions and mechanisms—in this case, not just whether one particular form of pricing "works," but rather why and how discounting works more broadly.

8
Shrouded Fees at StubHub

In 2016, Greg Mankiw, a renowned macroeconomist, took to the pages of the *New York Times* to talk about the high price of tickets to the musical *Hamilton* on Broadway. Mankiw wasn't complaining about the prices, which could exceed $1,000 per ticket, however, or about the fact that performances were regularly selling out despite the exorbitant cost. Instead, Greg was lauding the opportunity to buy scalped tickets for his family for $2,500 each on StubHub. The title of his article? "I Paid $2,500 for a 'Hamilton' Ticket. I'm Happy About It."[1]

Greg was making a point that many economists would at least partially agree with. Here's the backstory, which helps to explain how ticket resale markets can be a good thing. He purchased his family's *Hamilton* tickets on StubHub two days before the performance. An online marketplace, StubHub facilitates peer-to-peer resale of tickets to games, concerts, theaters, and other live events. On StubHub, sellers can try to resell tickets they purchased or otherwise acquired. Sometimes they can sell them for far more than the original sale price, sometimes for less, depending on demand.

Some people believe that those who resell tickets in this manner are behaving unethically. After all, the artists and others who pour their hard work and sweat into a production or game shouldn't be cheated out of these added profits. Others argue against ticket resales on the grounds that more people should have access to theater and other events without being pressured to cash out by selling their tickets. But Greg argued that markets like StubHub increase economic efficiency by connecting buyers and sellers who might otherwise have no way of reaching each other. This reasoning reflects a core principle of economics: trade between two people can make both sides better off, and markets are generally a good way to organize economic activities. In this case, Greg was happier paying $2,500 to see *Hamilton* than he would have been skipping it and saving the money. "It was only because the price was so high that I was able to buy tickets at all on such short notice," Greg writes. "If legal restrictions or moral sanctions had forced prices to remain close to face value, it is likely that no tickets would have been available by the time my family got around to planning its trip to the city." The previous owner of the tickets was presumably happier with the $2,500 than she would have been seeing the musical (or not seeing the musical, if she couldn't make it for some reason) and forgoing the $2,500. StubHub is making these types of transactions easier to do.

More generally, Greg's argument epitomizes the central role of market efficiency in the worldview of economics. In recent decades, economics has evolved to consider not only whether markets are efficient, but also how to design them to make them more efficient—and more profitable. We'll see that behavioral economics plays a role in guiding these decisions and that the outcome can be good or bad for customers, depending on the incentives of the company.

In this chapter, we'll consider the types of decisions StubHub has to make when designing its market—and the central role experiments play in these decisions. We'll see that important variables can get lost in these explorations of efficiency and profit: long-term financial outcomes and the potential harm a policy decision might inflict on outsiders.

To Shroud Fees or Not to Shroud?

On StubHub, a resale platform owned by eBay, individual sellers have the discretion to set their own ticket prices (with some constraints). Those prices can be higher or lower than the face value of the ticket. In addition to the price of the ticket itself, buyers pay fees to cover shipping, handling, and StubHub's service charge. In 2015, when the eBay team was thinking about this issue, buyers paid a 15% service charge per ticket, plus shipping and handling, the price of which could vary.[2]

StubHub faced a strategic decision: when and how should users be made aware of these fees? Since 2013, StubHub had used an "upfront fee" pricing strategy, which showed consumers the final price of the ticket, including all fees, from the moment they first saw the ticket inventory. This is in contrast to a "backend fee" strategy (which they had previously employed), in which customers would initially see only the price the seller charged and be made aware of additional fees only after selecting their ticket and navigating to the final checkout screen.

StubHub heavily marketed its upfront fee approach to pricing with ad tag lines such as "NO SURPRISE FEES AT CHECKOUT." The potential appeal of this straightforward approach was clear: Who hasn't been annoyed by hidden fees? That said, this didn't necessarily mean that StubHub was making the most *profitable* choice. Would reducing the salience of fees by obscuring them until the checkout page increase buyers' willingness to pay? After all, a growing body of behavioral economics had suggested that demand often depends not only on the total price, but on how salient different components of price are.[3]

Looking to turn these ideas into a prescription, economists Tom Blake, Sarah Moshary, Kane Sweeney, and Steve Tadelis (who were all on eBay's research team at the time) set out to understand whether an upfront or backend fee strategy would be more profitable for the company. The team was broadly tasked with using insights and tools from the field of economics to inform the design of eBay and its subsidiaries. Given prior research suggesting that hiding add-on fees could increase customer's willingness to pay, it seemed plausible that not revealing add-on fees until the last step in the purchasing process could induce buyers to spend more on StubHub—an outcome that the company clearly cared about. At the same time, the magnitude of the effect was unclear and the change risked alienating customers who valued the existing transparent approach.

An experiment was in order. In the final two weeks of August 2015, StubHub ran an experiment in which some users were shown tickets with upfront fees—StubHub's status quo policy—while others were shown tickets with backend fees. Users in the upfront fee condition were shown the final checkout price from their first viewing of the ticket, while users in the backend fee condition were shown the final price only after navigating to the last checkout page.

As in many of the experiments we've discussed, there were important managerial questions involved. Ultimately, StubHub would have to decide what data they should look at, what outcomes they care about, and how they should think about making a decision based on the results that would come in. Should they only think about profit? If not, what else should they take into account? We'll get to the results in a minute. But first, imagine that the experiment is still being planned; take a minute and write down your thoughts on how StubHub should proceed. What data should the research team be focusing on, and what criteria should the managers at StubHub use when deciding whether to switch to backend fees? Before reading on, remember that we are professors. This is your home-work. Please do answer these questions before reading further.

The Results

What data did you think StubHub should consider? Did you think about whether the research team should look at whether customers made the purchase? How about how much they paid? What about StubHub's profitability? What about long-term considerations, such as whether hidden fees would affect customers' likelihood of using the platform in the future? When planning an experiment, it's helpful to think about questions like these beforehand, which can help you avoid the temptation to contort the results after the data comes in.

StubHub ran the experiment for ten days (not an atypical length of time for an experiment in the tech sector) and tracked a few main metrics, including whether each user ended up making a pur-chase and, if so, how much they paid. The results were striking. Users exposed to backend fees were 13% more likely to purchase a ticket during a visit to StubHub than users exposed to upfront fees. Users exposed to backend fees spent 5.42% more than their upfront fee counterparts, a result that suggests people were buying better, higher-priced tickets when the fees were hidden.

So far, these results look clear-cut for StubHub—at least, if all the company cares about is short-term profit: Customers are more likely to purchase tickets and spend more when fees are tacked on at the end. But there's more to the story—and this is why it's important to track a broader set of metrics. The team found that while users paid more per ticket when fees were shrouded, they were somewhat less likely to come back to the website in the coming months—although this effect seems to be swamped by the increase in revenue from increased ticket sales and prices.

From Data to Decisions

Now that you know the results, it's time to make a decision. Should StubHub stay the course and maintain its transparent pricing policy or switch to a hidden fee regime? As we saw, the research team captured important and nuanced effects of tweaks to StubHub in their experiment. Next, StubHub had to figure out how to take the simple dependent variables that were studied (including the probability of a purchase, the amount spent per purchase, and the probability a customer would return for future purchases) and map them onto the deeper outcomes the company cared about, such as long-term profitability and growth.

While some downside to hiding fees emerged, the overall effect—at least in terms of profit—was positive. Without the experiment, StubHub would not have learned that the benefits of shrouding fees outweighed the costs, at least in terms of short-term profit.

But while the results suggest that shrouding is the most profitable business choice based on the available data, it's easy to see why the company might still be uncomfortable making the switch to hiding fees—even from a purely business perspective. First, like many experiments, this one mainly captures relatively short-term effects. In the long term, users may leave StubHub altogether if awareness grows of the new shrouding regime and its effects. This is a chronic problem faced by experimentalists ranging from managers at companies like StubHub and Google to policymakers in the federal government: Almost always, it is easier (and, by definition, faster) to capture short-term outcomes, whereas most leaders care at least as much about long-term outcomes.

When running experiments, it's worth thinking carefully about the relationship between short- and long-term outcomes, and also to invest more heavily in long-term outcomes. For example, we've helped tech companies create tools to help understand the relationship between short-term user metrics—most notably, clicks on the website—and longer-term, deeper behavioral changes of users, such as clicks on a restaurant's Yelp listing and ultimately the restaurant's revenues. To its credit, StubHub tracked one year's worth of outcomes for users who saw the shrouded fees. However, the experiment itself did not run for very long, and it might take time for the company to develop a negative reputation for shrouding and for the market effects of the new policy to fully play out. Moreover, reputational damage that might result from shrouding has the potential to affect both the control and the treatment group, meaning that it might be missed in the experiment. To be clear, this was an impressive and managerially relevant experiment, run by a top-notch team of economists. But even so, this is where managerial judgment needs to weigh the strengths and limitations of any experiment, its design, and the data that are currently available.

Experiments can provide unprecedented insight into the tradeoffs an organization may face as a result of a business decision. At the same time, they have the potential to lead decision makers to focus on short-term optimization and miss long-term risks (which tend to be harder to measure). This is a major challenge faced by companies running experiments. More generally, the value of an experiment is limited by the outcomes you are able to measure. Fortunately, there are ways to mitigate this limitation—in fact, this is exactly what the researchers had in mind when tracking longer-term outcomes. Similarly, StubHub could collect data aimed at measuring its reputation among people in different conditions. The company might track the number of complaints it receives and what they're about, the favorability of press coverage over time, and so on—none of these are perfect, but might give a fuller picture of the situation.

Ultimately, StubHub decided to adhere to the results of its experiment and change its "no surprise fees" policy. In a sharp shift from its bold commitment to transparency, the website now simply states, "StubHub is the world's top destination for ticket buyers and resellers. Prices may be higher or lower than face value."

In the near term, StubHub is almost certain to benefit in the form of increased profits. But the long-term effect of the new policy is still hard to predict. If StubHub wanted to shed more light on this issue, it could rerun the experiment with a third condition, one in which customers learn upfront that fees would be tacked on at the end. If the results showed that customers were turned off by that message (as evidenced by them leaving the platform or not making a purchase), that might suggest a longer-term risk to the company's brand.

Experiments are a valuable tool for improving companies' performance and facilitating better decision making. When incentives are aligned between a company and its customers or employees, experiments can create a lot of value for all parties involved. But there are also situations in which the value to customers or employees seems less clear, raising the potential for companies to gain financially at the expense of others. In those situations, it is up to companies to decide how to weigh financial profit against other factors, such as company reputation and customer satisfaction.

9

Market-Level Experiments at Uber

Life in the Internet age has introduced new information, new ways of making decisions, new ways of connecting to people, and even entirely new markets, like Airbnb and Uber. In the case of Uber, a new market was created with an app that matches riders with drivers. Designing a market from scratch is complicated, both because it's hard to match people at this scale and because there is no shortage of tradeoffs that the market designer (in this case, Uber) needs to make. Rideshare customers yearn for speedier, cheaper, or more convenient travel (and in many cases, all three). Rideshare drivers want swifter methods of obtaining more riders, higher wages, and a rider who won't eat a tuna sandwich in the backseat.

Uber, then, has a tough question on its hands: how best to match these folks in a way that suits their different goals—how best to link riders with drivers, or, in the case of a product like Uber Express Pool (a carpooling service), how best to match riders with both drivers and other riders. This isn't easy. Drivers have different schedules and aims; different cities come with different travel expectations; riders have different budgets, destinations, and timeframes, and, when pooling rides, they're often starting from different locations.

Like many of the tech companies we've discussed over the past few chapters, Uber runs thousands of experiments each year to shed light on such issues. To its credit, Uber has a sophisticated team of PhD economists and data scientists dedicated to understanding the vast data made available by digital interactions to help design a well-functioning marketplace. Uber has sought to experiment systematically with every aspect of product development, from the initial design and launch to evaluation and refinement. In this chapter, we'll explore an experiment that the company ran to decide whether or not to launch a new product, Uber Express Pool.

How Uber Experiments (and Why It's Challenging): The Case of Uber Express Pool

Open your Uber app (or your ridesharing app of choice) for a minute. As you know, you can request the standard taxi-like service, but with a regular car (e.g., UberX). You also have other options: UberXL, if you're traveling with a few friends or family members; UberSelect, if you prefer to ride in a fancier car (we've ridden with Uber drivers who drive Teslas); or UberPool, if you don't mind picking up and dropping off other riders along the way (you still get door-to-door service, but the trip takes a bit longer).

In 2018, Uber set out to understand whether to roll out a new product it was calling Uber Express Pool. With Express Pool, riders wait a little longer and walk a little farther to get to their destination. While they wait, a pool of riders (to be picked up at designated "express" meeting spots) is matched by an algorithm. The result is a carpool experience that might take longer but should save riders money (sometimes a lot of money, since they are now sharing the cost of the ride across multiple riders *and* riders are walking to a meeting spot) while making the trip more straightforward for their driver.

Yet, when we spoke to Duncan Gilchrist, a PhD economist and manager on Uber's rider-pricing and marketplace-experimentation data science team, he told us that it's a "really complicated thing" to measure and understand the effects of Express Pool. Most notably, experiments in marketplaces struggle to overcome spillover effects—in this case, the fact that if some, but not all, riders (or drivers) in a market can use Uber Express Pool, the entire market will be affected, ultimately biasing the results of the experiment. Thus, Uber's data science teams cannot always so simply run experiments by varying conditions across riders or drivers within a market. In a market of Uber riders, if a subset of people are given some treatment of interest (a new sort of pricing, or a new approach to carpooling), that would likely affect those in the control group as well (such as some earlier pricing model or other approach to carpooling), because the two riders are in the same market, being serviced by the same set of drivers.

Looking at the problem of spillover effects more closely, consider that Uber experiments frequently with its matching algorithms. Suppose that Uber were to assign half of Bostonian riders to a new algorithm, one that might increase riders' chances of finding rides. The other half of Bostonians would be a poor control group for this experiment, since their experience would be affected by the treatment as well—likely it would get worse as a result of all the cars now going to the riders in the treatment group. In this case, a new algorithm that led to small gains for the treatment group but large losses for the control group could look like a success on paper, but implementing that algorithm would be a bad idea overall.

Another complication is that the rollout of a new product can affect *all* Uber products. Uber thus needs to track not just what's happening in Express Pool, but how Express Pool affects UberX, UberXL, and Uber Pool. Suppose that a new algorithm were to improve performance in UberX (Uber's standard service). This might look like a success if it didn't reduce demand for other products. If this higher-performing UberX were simply taking riders away from UberBlack (Uber's premium service), the new algorithm might still be worth pursuing, but it would be less profitable than its initial appearance might have suggested. For such reasons, companies in the tech sector have to think carefully about their full suite of products.

Beyond Uber, examples abound:

- When Yelp improves its ability to facilitate deliveries to customers, it should check not only what happens to deliveries, but also what happens to the number of reservations made through the platform to see whether the improved delivery product crowds out other products.

- When Airbnb tweaks its "business travel" product, it should check not only how use of that product changes but how it affects the standard Airbnb listing product.

- When Amazon experiments with its online shopping experience, a large change in shopping behavior would alter the entire way that users engage with the platform—so Amazon would also want to see whether the experiment changed the number of users who were streaming movies.

- This concern goes well beyond the tech sector. Recall the Campbell's Soup example from the 1970s that we discussed in chapter 4, in which the company was worried about whether its new semi-condensed Soup for One would crowd out its other soups.

Uber thinks carefully about experiments and has doubled down on using them to understand core questions such as what products to launch, where to launch them, and how to design them. To avoid spillover effects and understand how a new product is affecting its entire portfolio, Uber tends to run market-level experiments for some of its bigger changes, in which a product is rolled out in a randomly selected subset of markets, but to all users within that market. For instance, a product might be rolled out in all of Cleveland and not at all in Boston, making Boston the control group. In the case of Uber Express Pool, Uber selected a set of large markets and rolled out the product in six cities that were randomly selected from this set.

Leveraging recent advances in experimental methods—especially a statistical method that allowed Uber to use a weighted combination of other cities to form a more suitable "synthetic" control group—Duncan and his team were able to tease out the ways in which the rollout was influencing Uber usage. Unsurprisingly, Express Pool created new kinds of trip matches. But the experiment also accounted for the effect of Express Pool on existing Uber products and made clear that launching it would make good business sense. As a result, Uber was able confidently to introduce Express Pool to many of its major markets. This confidence, and the finding that inspired it, would not have been possible without the experiment.

Express Pool was a big win for Uber (and for Max personally; Mike still prefers UberX—though UberSelect is a worthwhile splurge when it is available during his travels). But Duncan and his team haven't called it a day with this experiment. They continue to experiment with the myriad factors that might further improve this product. In a complicated world with many products, Uber has invested heavily in an experimental approach. "It's where experimentation really shines brightly," Duncan says. "You can imagine running experiments where we just change, in a given city, the wait time that riders are asked to wait—from, say, two to four minutes—and measure what happens to the overall market when you do that." There's a lot of data for the experimenters to consider. Uber serves hundreds of cities, and Duncan points out that the "right set of parameters is probably different city by city, which makes experimentation all the more challenging."

The effects of all these variables, all these different contexts, can be kind of amazing. "The right tradeoff is probably different in the suburbs versus in a city," Duncan says, "and it's probably different during rush hour versus non-rush hour." There's so much to experiment with and so many things to measure. The so-muchness of it all is why economists trained in this kind of experimentation are suited for companies like Uber. The beauty of Uber's data-driven approach is its elucidation of that range of factors, which allows Uber to know whether and how to offer a product like Express Pool.

Ultimately, Duncan's experiments demonstrated that Express Pool was, in fact, a valuable addition to Uber's suite of services. Perhaps more important, the experiments allowed the company to understand how best to develop a new product in a dynamic and complicated market with a suite of other products, all within a competitive landscape where a rider might be choosing not just between Uber products but between taking an Uber, a Lyft, a taxi, a bus, a train, a car, a bike, or a walk.

These experiments help to illustrate more broadly the ways in which experiments fit into the process of innovation. At Uber, the innovation process often starts with lower-cost data gathering—including discussions with users, analyses of historical data and the current market, and running simulations to get a sense of what might happen if they were to make a change. For new products that they want to push forward, Uber will often pilot the change in one or two cities—essentially to make sure the product is functioning as expected (i.e., that nothing completely breaks). Companies have long used these forms of data gathering. Uber builds on this by running large market-level experiments, followed by smaller experiments aimed at refining the product—and then iterates on the whole process as necessary.

Over time, Duncan and his colleagues at Uber have continued to refine the innovation process, making sure that they are leveraging the potential of experiments to improve the company's products. Market-level experiments have been important, but are also complicated to run—and limit the total number of experiments that

Uber can run. At the same time, they give the company the best idea of how markets will evolve in the wake of a product change or launch—especially when the experiment can be run for a long enough period of time. The company has increasingly leaned on market-level experiments for its most important changes, which has helped it to overcome some of the problems that tech experiments often face.

The series of experiments that Duncan's team ran for this project are just a few of the thousands the company runs each year to test everything from pricing tweaks to new products to changes in their review system. For example, Uber ran a series of experiments to study the impact of allowing tipping. The experiments found that few people used the tipping option and that tipping played little role in driver behavior, which is different from the large impact some economists were predicting. Another series of experiments by Basil Halperin, Benjamin Ho, John List, and Ian Muir looked at drivers' apologies for late rides and found that giving a small coupon after a bad experience could lead to increased future use while "an apology without a promotion (i.e., words alone) had no effect or was even sometimes counterproductive."

Tech companies have quickly realized the value of the economics toolkit for experimentation, and they have been snapping up PhD economists on an impressive scale. A growing set of economists, like Duncan, are opting for careers in tech even when doors are opening for them at the most rarefied heights of academia. Duncan received a Harvard PhD in business economics, a joint program between Harvard's economics department and business school (where Mike was one of his advisors). He published chapters from his dissertation in leading academic journals, and his research covered areas ranging from patents and drug innovation to network effects in movie-going. Duncan would have been a great candidate for an academic job at a top business school. And he enjoyed his studies, but, he says, "I was also itching to do more of this physical-world style of stuff." He wanted "to do more than write papers." So he made his way to Wealthfront (a financial technology company investing heavily in using behavioral economics to improve customer decision making) and then to Uber, where he now manages a team of more than fifty people who spend their days running experiments, using a combination of data, technical expertise, creativity, and managerial skills.

Economists have long played a central role in government and business, from helping to shape economic policy in the President's Council of Economic Advisors to developing a pricing system at major airlines to providing expert testimony in labor and discrimination disputes. Even so, the rise of economists in tech has been unique. Major companies, including Amazon, eBay, Google, Microsoft, Facebook, Airbnb, and Uber, have large teams of PhD economists working to engineer better design choices. Outnumbering the largest university economics departments, Amazon now has more than 100 PhD economists. As discussed in chapter 3, such economists have played an important role in tech experiments because of the tech sector's ability to avoid barriers that hold other companies back from rigorous experimentation. These economists, in turn, have helped to provide theoretical grounding for the design and interpretation of tech experiments, and guidance on how and when to invest in experiments.

10

The Facebook Blues

Are you a Facebook user? If so, open your account for a minute. We'll wait. Now look at your News Feed, the thing going down the center of your screen. What do you see? A post from an old friend, perhaps. A shared news story. An advertisement. Now think about the many, many things Facebook could have placed in your feed. It could have shown you any post from any of your hundreds of Facebook connections. It could have shown you any news story in the world or a wide variety of ads. Yet it chose to show you precisely what's sitting in front of you right now.

Those selections are no accident. Facebook uses an algorithm that sifts through everything the company knows about you, everything that is going on with your friends and family, and all the news happening around the world to decide which posts to show you and how long they should linger in your feed before falling into oblivion.

Facebook takes this Herculean task seriously. The News Feed team's engineers, data scientists, and economists spend their work hours thinking about things like whether to show you more articles about the latest US trade negotiations with China or more pictures of your aunt's pecan pie. OK, maybe that one's easy. Pecan pie is pretty amazing—and, we recently realized, relatively straightforward to make from scratch. Plus, you need to know whether your aunt somehow managed to line up the pecans in concentric circles or just lazily scattered them around the pie. (We personally try for concentric circles but end up with messy scatterings. If you have a tip for ensuring concentric circles, please contact us.)

Getting back to Facebook, the News Feed received considerable attention after the 2016 US election, when it came to light that the platform had unwittingly featured news stories, many of them favoring Donald Trump, that turned out to be fake. Not only were the stories fake, but US intelligence agencies report that they were created by a "troll farm" in Russia, likely at the behest of Russian president Vladimir Putin in an effort to sway the election in Trump's direction.[1] Fake news accounted for roughly 1% of stories shared through Facebook during the election cycle. There was little comfort for Facebook—not to mention its users—in learning that these mini-firebombs probably hadn't been prevalent enough to be the deciding factor in the election; the damage to the company's reputation had been done. So Facebook made a series of changes to the News Feed, such as vetting articles, removing those determined to be false, and barring providers of fake content.

Dealing with fake news is just one of many challenges Facebook's News Feed team faces on a day-to-day basis. For example, should it prioritize news stories or pictures? The *New York Times* or blogs? Close friends (whose news you might already know) or acquaintances (whose updates may be less directly important to you, but more "newsworthy" to you since you might not have heard about them already)? How prevalent should ads be?

We all have opinions about these questions, but Facebook would prefer to minimize the guesswork involved in understanding how its News Feed will affect its bottom line. Like Uber, it has worked to refine its innovation process over the years. According to Facebook economist Alex Peysakovich and former Googler

Seth Stephens-Davidowitz, this process includes "an old-fashioned approach: asking. Every day, hundreds of individuals load their News Feed and answer questions about the stories they see there. Big data (likes, clicks, comments) is supplemented by small data ('Do you want to see this post in your News Feed?') and contextualized ('Why?')."[2]

It also heavily features experiments, which the company runs thousands of per year. Odds are that if you are a regular Facebook user, you are also a regular participant in its many experiments. Some of these experiments tweak your News Feed content, tracking its effect on your engagement with the platform. Others are aimed at learning which advertisements you will click on. Still others are geared toward figuring out the best overall layout of the website (such as the size of the font). And one experiment in particular looked at the effects of happy and sad posts on users' moods—with results that Facebook didn't anticipate.

The Debbie Downer Effect

When Adam Kramer, a Facebook data scientist, started wondering whether happy and sad posts affect users' moods, the company decided to use its experimental apparatus to find out. Working with researchers Jamie Guillory and Jeffrey Hancock from Cornell University, Kramer started by looking at more than 600,000 users and tweaking their feeds. Our interviews suggest that the experiment was conducted mainly out of curiosity—that Facebook had no immediate plans to change the News Feed as a result of the findings. The experimenters randomly selected some of these users and showed them mostly happy posts from their Facebook friends, as measured by words and phrases used in their text, such as "My vacation was sweet," or "One hell of a pecan pie—excited!" Another set of randomly selected users was not so lucky. These subjects were shown a feed full of gloomy, negative posts from those they knew, such as "This bird seed is worthless. Just found out my canary is allergic to it. ☹"

The researchers then tracked the new posts of those being studied to observe whether they were more likely to write positive or negative things after seeing more positive or negative posts, respectively, from their friends.

The experiment reminds us of the now-classic Debbie Downer skit from the 2004 season of *Saturday Night Live*. When offered steak and eggs on a trip to Disney World, a character played by Rachel Dratch replies, "Ever since they found mad cow disease in the US, I'm not taking any chances. It can live in your body for years before it ravages your brain."[3] The statement, accented by the sound of a muted trumpet, leaves Debbie's friends depressed. The emotion experiment was essentially a test of whether the Debbie Downer effect exists on Facebook.

The result? The Debbie Downers of Facebook do dampen our moods, but only slightly—at least according to the measures described in the paper: if a user was exposed to the negative post condition, she ended up writing about four additional negative words out of every 10,000 words she wrote. And if a user was exposed to the positive post condition, she ended up writing seven fewer negative words out of every 10,000 words she wrote. As context, a typical *New York Times* op-ed contains fewer than 1,000 words. So, relative to someone in the positive treatment, someone in the negative treatment would write about one additional negative word per op-ed worth of writing.

Mad, Not Sad

When they published their findings, the researchers learned something else as well: that people were shocked and upset to hear about Facebook's manipulation of emotional content in the name of experimentation.[4] "They didn't do right by their customers," a Gartner analyst told the *New York Times*.[5] Media reports were full of criticism, with headlines such as these:

- "Facebook Reveals News Feed Experiment to Control Emotions"—*The Guardian*
- "Everything We Know About Facebook's Secret Mood Manipulation"—*The Atlantic*
- "Facebook Conducted Secret Psychology Experiment on Users' Emotions"—*The Telegraph*

Some people flatly said this sort of psychological manipulation is ethically impermissible under all circumstances. Others said the researchers should have been required to get subjects' consent. And while some of the concerns were warranted, others were misguided.

Take the first criticism, that influencing user emotions is impermissible under any circumstances. In fact, advertisers and other groups manipulate consumers' emotions all the time to suit their purposes. If you've ever read a Hallmark card, attended a football game, or seen a commercial for the ASPCA, you've been exposed to the myriad ways in which products and services influence consumers' emotions. Maybe we're emotionally fragile, but even that popular Internet meme of a Shiba Inu with a funny look and an inner dialogue in broken English tugs at our heartstrings.[6] (Note: We just checked with our spouses and it turns out that, yes, we are emotionally fragile. Nonetheless, we think our broader point stands.) *Of course* our emotions are influenced by the content we see! And our News Feeds are no different. Facebook posts inevitably influence your emotions—and it's often the emotional content that makes them interesting and engaging. Now, maybe users don't like posts that make them sad, but the number of sad (relative to happy) posts you see is affected by every design choice Facebook makes, whether intentionally or not. And it's hard to imagine people wanting Facebook to ban sad posts altogether.

So, Facebook had two options. Like the pre-experimentation UK Revenue and Customs authority described in chapter 1, it could have remained behind a veil of ignorance, making no effort to understand the emotional impact of its decisions. Or the company could have tried to assess the results of its decisions in the hope of someday using the information to make better design choices. Facebook chose the latter.

OK, fine. But what about the consent issue? Shouldn't Facebook have emailed (or, we suppose, poked) users, offering them the chance to opt in to this experiment, rather than assuming that everyone would be fine with it? After all, social science researchers must get participants' consent for lab experiments.

Actually, consent is the norm in labs, but social scientists in real-world settings such as workplaces and street corners routinely conduct certain types of experiments without getting consent. The Institutional Review Boards that monitor human experiments in universities can explicitly waive the consent requirement for field studies when the protocols are mostly harmless, for the very good reason that focusing attention on the experiment can also skew the results. In one experiment, for example, Mike and his colleagues hired hundreds of people to work at the online-work platform oDesk to gauge employees' level of effort in response to varying amounts of pay. The work assigned to these people was real, and the study presented minimal risk. In this situation, the IRB didn't require the research team to inform the participants that they were part of an experiment.

Things get a little murkier in the Facebook case. At the time, Facebook didn't have a review board to tell its researchers whether or not to seek consent. So, when deciding whether to seek consent, they went with a resounding *sort of*. If you use Facebook, then technically you *have* consented to being a subject in its experiments.

You know those pages and pages of fine-print terms of service that you attested to having read when you signed up on Facebook? Yeah, those. The ones you agreed to. Without reading. (Research estimates that it would take you 76 eight-hour days to read the privacy policies of the websites you visit.)[7] Somewhere in that eye-straining mass of words, you "acknowledged" that Facebook has the right to use your personal information for testing and research. After the brouhaha over its emotion experiment, Facebook updated its terms of service to state: "We conduct surveys and research, test features in development, and analyze the information we have to evaluate and improve products and services, develop new products or features, and conduct audits and troubleshooting activities." This situation highlights the need for companies to publish clear guidelines about when and how users will be informed about any experiments they are taking part in.

The worst part of the backlash against the emotion experiment was its effect on Facebook. Before the experiment went public, Facebook had been an outlier among corporations at the time, in that it had publicly reported some of its more interesting experiments (just a few of many thousands of experiments, but still). In response to the outcry over the emotion study, the company stopped publicizing the results of its experiments altogether for a period of time—though it didn't stop running them. Other companies likely took away the same message: transparency is dangerous, and experiments are best kept under wraps. Facebook has now started reporting some of its results again, with a beefed-up review process.

Toward Greater Transparency

What was it about Facebook's experiment that got under people's skin? What red line did Facebook cross?

The problem was that media reports of the experiment made it sound, to many people, like the workings of a mad scientist, straight out of *Orphan Black*: Facebook, a trusted friend, had toyed with their emotions for an *experiment*. This sounds bad. But suppose that Facebook had been even more transparent with users about all of its ongoing research into how the News Feed affects people. Suppose it had said something like, "As we do every year now, we ran roughly 500 experiments last year aimed at better understanding user preferences and improving the content displayed in the News Feed. We ran experiments on a number of dimensions—including whether to prioritize posts from your local friends or more distant ones, whether to leave posts for a long period of time or only briefly (allowing you to see more total posts), and whether to prioritize positive posts or negative ones. We learned a lot through the process, including the fact that if we prioritize positive posts, readers of the posts tend to also start writing happier posts (though the effect size is tiny). See the highlights of the results from other experiments on our results blog. Please email us if you have other suggestions for improving the News Feed or our tests, so that we can incorporate them into future research and development of the News Feed."

With this type of greater transparency, the findings about the emotional-contagion research would have been demystified and described in plain English—and they might not have faced an angry backlash. Our takeaway from the story isn't that companies shouldn't publish their experimental results. It's that they should be publishing (whether formally in research journals or in blog posts) a lot *more* of their findings in an attempt to be transparent with customers.

Secrecy is a bigger danger than publicity. Recall the Airbnb experiment in chapter 4, in which one of Mike's experiments uncovered discrimination on the lodging-rental platform. Airbnb's initial response was to avoid the topic like the plague. Later, the company was criticized for its denial of the problem and lack of action.

Airbnb might well have been better off addressing the issue from the get-go through transparency and design changes.

More generally, instead of hiding their experimentation (or burying explanations in user agreements that no one reads), companies should embrace the experimental method and establish a transparent process to clarify their engagement in it. Such efforts might include the following goals:

- Acknowledge, in broad terms, that the company frequently creates experiments to gauge people's responses (and, yes, to take those responses to the bank);

- Explain the value of experiments to the company and to the public;

- To the extent possible, encourage discussion of the company's experimental aims and methods (this can be difficult in some contexts, as some companies view their experimental infrastructure as an advantage that they would like to hide from competitors); and,

- When appropriate, be transparent about the experiments' findings. (As we'll discuss below, companies do far more experiments than they can possibly detail, so they would have to be selective. And, as above, these results can be an advantage that companies might want to hide from competitors, which can also make sharing difficult.)

Companies might also consider posting (or at least keeping track of) information about their experiments. Facebook, for example, now posts about some of its research.[8] One rule of thumb might be to focus transparency efforts on experiments that could lead to major or controversial changes in the company's policies or offerings, or those that might meaningfully harm some users. A company like Facebook could even go as far as educating individual users about their research participation, perhaps through annual notifications, such as "Last year, you were involved in 17 of our experiments. Three of these involved your News Feed."

Today, almost all tech companies run experiments, and they will continue to do so. They have to: experimentation is their lifeblood. They need to continually try out features, products, design, messaging, packaging, and interfaces to see what works and what doesn't. These experiments are valuable not only to the companies but also to users, who presumably don't want low-quality services as a result of gut decisions that could easily have been improved through data.

This means that users should be open to experimentation, and companies should stop shrouding the process in secrecy and mishandling communication surrounding their experimentation. Consumers are smart: they know that companies tinker with changes in products and services and assess customers' reactions. Companies should be held to high standards for transparency and ethics in experimentation. In turn, if they are candid about their research, they will be able to defuse suspicion, enlist support, and perhaps even deepen customer engagement.

Broader Lessons from Tech Experiments

The Internet age has made life better in a variety of ways. We can now sit on the couch eating pizza we ordered through Yelp, while binge-watching the last season of *Luke Cage* on Netflix and scrolling through Amazon to order a pair of noise-cancelling headphones with one-day delivery to use on a long-haul flight the next evening—not that we're speaking from experience.

But while these platforms have brought incredible convenience and efficiency to our lives, it can also be challenging to figure out how to best leverage the products they've offered. No one grapples with this challenge more than the companies themselves—many of which manage complex interactions in the online world. Often, companies' goals are to make life better offline, although sometimes companies make choices that may leave us worse off. And in all of these cases, experiments play a central role in guiding the decisions companies make and how they affect us.

From the experiments we've explored in part II, we can glean a number of lessons that are applicable to experimentation both within the tech sector and beyond. Here are six of them:

- Lesson 1: Experimentation can help to complement intuition with data, leading to large gains, as we saw in the case of eBay advertising.

- Lesson 2: Experiments often serve at least one of four key purposes:
  - Testing theory and mechanisms,
  - Understanding magnitudes and tradeoffs,
  - Evaluating specific policies or products,
  - Exploratory fact finding, in cases where you don't have a theory.

- Lesson 3: It's often helpful to think about a series of experiments as a way to develop a framework, rather than using a single experiment to ask and answer an important business question.

- Lesson 4: Experiments can at times lead to a focus on overly narrow or short-term outcomes—those that are top of mind and easily measured. Companies can benefit from being explicit about the broader set of outcomes they care about and thinking about the map between the outcomes they have and the outcomes they care most about.

- Lesson 5: Technical challenges—such as spillover effects—can dramatically affect the interpretation and accuracy of experiments. There are often good technical solutions, but this requires thinking carefully about the implementation details of experiments.

- Lesson 6: Experiments are often hidden from the public. Increased transparency has the potential to foster better communication between companies and customers about the decisions they make.

In part III, we'll return from the tech sector to behavioral experiments like the ones we saw in part I. We'll focus on the broader diffusion of behavioral experiments—thinking about how different organizations and sectors began to develop a culture of experimentation. We'll give a sense of the types of behavioral experiments that are occurring throughout health, education, and financial decision making. Throughout, we'll draw out lessons for why experiments were influential in these settings, and the roles they have played.

Part III   Experimenting for the Social Good

11

Behavioral Experiments for the Social Good

As we've noted, the tech sector was an early adopter of a culture of experimentation. But, as we mentioned in chapter 2, long before the experimental revolution in tech (and before the tech era), governments dabbled in the idea of experimentally testing social programs—running experiments on everything from who gets insurance to where people live. More recently, we've seen experiments start to diffuse and scale in a growing set of sectors. To get a sense of how organizations are thinking about scaling an experimental approach and creating a culture of experimentation, we'll return to the rise of behavioral insights units and think through their approach to creating a culture of experimentation. We'll then walk through the transition of "turn out the vote" operations from being largely the domain of leaders with big brands but little data to teams of experimentalists testing the approaches they were selling to political clients.

The Diffusion of Behavioral Insight Units

The UK Behavioural Insights Team was launched with the goal of making governments more efficient. The core ideas that formed the BIT toolkit came from the laboratory experiments of behavioral economics and the psychology of social influence, drawing on conceptual ideas from Cialdini, Kahneman, Tversky, Thaler, and others. But experimental testing also quickly became a central part of the behavioral insights movement, as organizations realized that (1) they needed to prove their value to skeptical stakeholders, (2) they didn't really know which insights would generalize to the settings they were interested in, and (3) the academic literature contained insufficient guidance for the problems they cared most about. (Of course, these are good reasons to experiment in areas well beyond behavioral insights.)

As new units cropped up, they often started with a pilot project that would allow them to show the returns they could provide, at times causing them to focus on testing interventions that they were pretty sure would be effective. For example, let's return to the tax letter example from chapter 1. When the UK team tested this letter, there was a lot of uncertainty about how impactful varying letters would be and whether they would meaningfully move the needle on repayment rates. As it turns out, they did—creating a big win for BIT. Over the years, units in other governments, which operated separately from BIT, often tested their own version of the tax letter. At some point, they went from being very uncertain that the tax letter would change behavior to being fairly certain that it would do something, even if the exact magnitude was unknown. Yet many units continued to replicate the initial tax letter experiment, finding qualitatively consistent results. They didn't keep running this experiment to find out whether the effect was 1% or 2%. Rather, they wanted to provide a proof of concept to show stakeholders that their unit could apply behavioral insights to their context in a way that would help improve their bottom line.

BIT also became a central organizing force for and provider of services to other emerging behavioral insights units, including helping other units launch their first trials. By 2017, there were dozens of behavioral insight teams based in local or federal governments around the world.

Countries are continuing to develop nudge units, and not-for-profits and consulting firms have entered the market. These units aim to achieve sustainable improvements to government operations, and they often do so by following the UK BIT's lead of using field experiments as the gold standard of evidence.

In 2014, along with the government of New South Wales, the Singaporean nudge unit, and Harvard's Behavioral Insights Group (which we are both affiliates of), the UK BIT organized an annual conference, focused on latest developments in the field, that has grown to attract up to 800 participants. Another active organization in bringing behavioral insights to the field is Ideas42, a social science research and development laboratory launched in June 2008 at Harvard by a cross-university group of scholars and the International Finance Corporation (a global development institution affiliated with the World Bank) with the goal of "using scientific insights to design innovative policies and products, both domestically and internationally." Soon after, Ideas42 was spun off into a not-for-profit aimed at generating new solutions in the areas of financial access for the poor, diffusion of more effective technologies for food harvesting in developing countries, health coverage in the United States, and educational opportunities in low-income communities. Often this work included running experiments. Though still a nonprofit, Ideas42 is a behavioral economics consulting firm in the mold of the UK BIT—in fact, the two tend to be viewed as competitors. The major for-profit consulting firms are keeping track of this new area of consulting, regularly attending the major meetings that are open to the public.

As these organizations proliferate, the multiple objectives of experimentation are clear. Experiments help organizations figure out what initiatives are effective and demonstrate their value to stakeholders. And, in these organizations, experiments have been used with the goal of achieving policy goals.

Transforming Advice on Getting Out the Vote

While organizations like BIT and Ideas42 have worked with policymakers to use experiments for the social good, experiments have also come to play a role much earlier in the political process—with getting people to vote. To get a sense of how turn-out-the-vote campaigns became enamored with experiments, it's helpful to have a sense of the broader landscape of voter behavior and turnout. Of course, people generally view voting as a positive behavior. In fact, as of 2004, some democracies even required their citizens to vote, including Australia, Brazil, and Argentina. In contrast, voter turnout in recent US presidential elections has ranged from 54% to 58%. Through the 2004 presidential election, plenty of "experts" offered campaigns paid advice on how to increase voting rates, despite often having very little evidence of the success of the strategies they offered, other than their (highly fallible) expert judgment.

Researchers have run many experiments to determine what leads citizens to vote. As far back as 1927, University of Chicago political scientist Harold Gosnell described a study, one of the earliest field experiments on record, in which Chicagoans randomly received cartoons depicting nonvoters as unpatriotic slackers.[1] For decades, the topic remained largely an academic one; professional pollsters and political scientists had limited connections.

This began to change in the 1990s, when Yale political scientists Alan Gerber and Donald Green began to examine what motivates people to vote. In 1998, as the mid-cycle November elections approached in the United States, Gerber and Green worked with the League of Women Voters to divide 30,000 New Haven citizens into four groups. Some citizens received large postcards encouraging them to vote. Others received the same message via a phone call. A third group received an in-person visit at their front door. A fourth group, the control group, was not contacted at all. After voting day in November 1998, Gerber and Green examined Connecticut records to see who actually voted. (Whom you voted for is not on the public record, but whether you voted is.) In-person canvassing increased turnout by 9.8% in comparison to voters who were not contacted. Mail only led to an increase of 0.6% in comparison to the control group, and telephone calls had no effect at all. When Gerber and Green published their work in 2010, some campaign operatives believed the academics were assailing their work,[2] while direct mail vendors selectively cited the research to argue that candidates would be wasting money on phone calls.

In 2003, a young Democratic pollster and recent Williams College graduate named Todd Rogers became excited about the potential for behavioral science to offer insight into the political process (and polling industry), and entered the doctoral program in social psychology at Harvard. He soon found the psychology program too restrictive to allow him to focus on the topic that drove him to grad school—how to get people to vote for Democrats—so he transferred within Harvard to the Organizational Behavioral program (a joint program between the Harvard Business School and the psychology and sociology departments in the Faculty of Arts and Sciences). With the switch, Max became Todd's lead adviser. Max views his willingness to get out of Todd's way and let him study how to get people to vote to be one of his main contributions to democracy.

In his new program, Todd worked on a series of papers with Wharton professor Katy Milkman (who was also Max's student at the time; we'll hear more about her in chapters 12 and 13) and Max about how to get people to do what they thought they "should" do rather than what they momentarily "want" to do, but he continued to be driven to understand how to get more people to vote.

In 2006, Craig Fox invited Max to come to New York for a meeting of Democratic-leaning social psychologists and behavioral economists. The group, which came to be known as the Consortium of Behavioral Scientists, helped Democrats apply the results of academic research to win elections and turn more of the electoral map blue. Max asked Craig if he could bring along a bright Harvard graduate student who was obsessed with the topic of the meeting—Todd. Craig agreed.

Those of us in the room soon ran into a problem: we knew very little about the election process. At one point, an eminent social psychologist who had only met Todd earlier in the day advised the group that we should probably stop pontificating and listen to Todd, who had on-the-ground knowledge from his days working on the issue. As a third-year graduate student, Todd's practical-minded interests made an important contribution to the consortium, which went on to have substantial influence on the successful 2008 presidential campaign of Barack Obama, as documented in Sasha Issenberg's book *The Victory Lab: The Secret Science of Winning Campaigns*.

As Todd continued with his dissertation research, he added Yale professor Alan Gerber to his dissertation committee due to his expertise in voting research (as described earlier). During Todd's final year in graduate school, in late 2007, he received an invitation to interview for a tenure-track position at the Harvard Kennedy School of Government, but he passed on this in order to accept a job in Washington, DC: Gerber had recommended him to be the founding executive director of the Analyst Institute, a left-leaning organization founded earlier that year by AFL-CIO officials and liberal allies. Inspired by the work of Green, Gerber, and others, the founders wanted to create an organization that would focus on using field experiments to establish a set of empirically proven best practices for interacting with voters. The group was well funded and offered Todd the opportunity to run field experiments on voting at a much more rapid clip than academia could provide, with an audience waiting to use his results. And the mission was in line with Todd's political goals of helping Democrats get elected.

Todd took the position and quickly rose to fame in Democratic political circles, as well as among those who believe that social science can be useful in improving voter turnout. Over the next few years, Todd was in the thick of more than 300 field experiments focused on how to get out the vote and also on increasing support for progressive candidates. Most were proprietary, the results accessible only to left-leaning groups associated with the Analyst Institute. "There seem to be two types of political operatives in Washington: those who think Rogers is a genius transforming their field and those who have never heard of him," wrote Issenberg in *The Victory Lab*.

A savvy operator with good political instincts, Todd was able to strategically use experiments to bring attention to his work and at times to disprove the intuition of the ruling class of political operatives he was competing against. Many campaign operatives didn't feel a need to connect to social science research, preferring to cling to their intuitions. Todd tried not to leave them much choice. At times, he would make stakeholders predict which approach to turning out the vote or persuading voters was best and then use experimental results to show them they were wrong (and occasionally right).

Like other experimentalists, one way in which Todd used experiments was to demonstrate the value of his organization's proposed changes. In April 2007, for instance, he created a script for phone calls made to 19,411 Democratic households in Pennsylvania in the lead-up to the state's presidential primary. In one of the experimental conditions, the implementation-intention condition, callers asked registered voters three questions: "Around what time do you expect you will head to the polls on Tuesday? Where do you expect you will be coming from when you head to the polls on Tuesday? What do you think you will be doing before you head out to the polls?" The goal was not to find the answer to these questions; rather, Rogers was testing whether citizens would be more likely to vote when they had thought through how to do so—when they'd made a plan. They were. The idea wasn't new to psychology—it was based on an idea called "implementation intentions," which was introduced by NYU psychology Peter Gollwitzer. The basic idea is that nudging people to make concrete plans has the potential to increase the likelihood of actually completing a goal. But Todd's experiment played an important role in helping political candidates fine-tune the idea in a way that could be applied to voter turnout and leveraged for their political gain.

Ultimately, Todd's experiments helped displace some of the old guard political consultants who went with their gut, while allowing him to adapt known insights to the context he cared about. He harvested results from social psychology and turned them into tools to improve voter turnout—and, in the process, transformed how campaigns are run in the United States.

By the fall of 2008, Todd's application of a plan-making strategy, as well as other insights he brought to Washington, became standard tools for many left-leaning candidates. He also applied Robert Cialdini's research on social norms, which shows that people act the way they see other people acting, to create call scripts that included lines such as, "Turnout is going to be high today." These strategies at times stood in sharp contrast to the strategy of Democratic presidential candidate John Kerry's campaign during the 2004 election of focusing on the fact that many Americans fail to vote. Todd's experiments showed that focusing on all the citizens who will be voting is much more effective than focusing on all those who will be skipping the opportunity to vote.[3]

Former Analyst Institute associates have now gone on to work for leading Democratic and progressive organizations, and many of the tools and scripts Todd and his colleagues created are now a small but recognized component of effective campaign strategy across the political divide.

Was this use of behavioral experiments to turn out the vote good for society? The answer may be yes for Obama fans, which highlights the nuances of behavioral experiments, even those aimed at improving the social good. As was the case here, "turning out the vote" often means "turning out the vote among those we think will vote for the person we want to win." For example, a partisan approach to turning out the vote might focus on encouraging voter turnout in left-leaning neighborhoods while ignoring right-leaning neighborhoods. While we are fans both of the Obama presidency and of Todd Rogers's research, we recognize the potential risks of leaving voting decisions to behavioral scientists working with a political agenda. Just as experiments help to make companies smarter, they helped to make Democratic efforts to turn out the vote more effective—and the extent to which this is a good thing depends on whether you think the Democratic Party's incentives are aligned with societal wellbeing. An alternative societal goal might be to see more nonpartisan organizations help to turn out the vote with the intent of making sure *all* voices are heard, rather than just those aligned with one political party.

12

Healthy, Wealthy, and Wise

While Todd Rogers's career as a political operative was a success, in large part due to his ability to succinctly distill social psychology insights into how-to guides for political campaigns looking for more votes, he missed doing the kind of research that would allow him to understand the psychological processes underlying a wider variety of behaviors and influence those behaviors. So he left DC and headed back to academia. Fortunately, the job that had interested him earlier in his career was still interested in him. Joining the Kennedy School of Government as an assistant professor in 2011 (in the department where Max is a faculty member), Todd wanted to shift the focus of his research from voting to other areas where behavioral science insights might have an outsize effect.

As it turns out, he joined the school at a time when a growing number of faculty shared this interest. Repeating his approach from his get-out-the-vote business, Todd decided to focus again on one core topic—but wasn't sure if it should be the environment or education. After dabbling in the world of environmental research, Todd settled on education as his new research interest—excited by the growing body of behavioral education research, the established community of researchers in this area, and the potential to have a direct impact on practice (at the time, schools were starting to line up to learn more about how to use behavioral insights to improve student outcomes).

Todd joined a burgeoning group of scholars who work with organizations to understand and shape decisions related to education, health, and finances. In this chapter, we'll give a taste of the work being done in these three areas and the lessons they offer experimentalists.

Wise

Ben Castleman and Lindsay Page first read *Nudge* when they were doctoral students at the Harvard Graduate School of Education. Both had worked in education, Ben as a school administrator and Lindsay as an education policy analyst at Abt Associates and a teacher before that. They had a deep understanding of the US education system and the challenges students face. In particular, they had become interested in the large number of high school students who might benefit from college but who were not going. Enrolling for college and then dropping out during the summer before college began was such a common phenomenon that it got its own name—"summer melt."

Passionate about reducing melt rates and undeterred by the scale of the problem, the pair embarked on an ambitious set of collaborations with schools and nonprofit organizations to use behavioral experiments to help students stay on the path toward college enrollment and completion and improved career prospects. In the summer of 2011, they launched their first experiment in collaboration with Fulton County Schools (in Georgia) and uAspire, a Boston-based organization dedicated to helping students get the mentoring and financial support they need. In the experiment, they randomly offered a subset of high school students from Boston and Fulton County college counseling from high school counselors or community-based financial aid advisors during the summer after high school graduation. In principle, all students could check in with their counselor or advisor, but the students in the treatment group were proactively contacted. The counselors could use anything from text to email to Facebook messaging to get in touch with students. If they did reach a student, they would help them review financial aid forms, remind students of important deadlines (such as tuition payment), and assess whether the student had social or emotional barriers to attending. The counselors spent about 2–3 hours with each student.

The results were striking. The intervention led to a 3% increase in the likelihood the student would enroll in college, suggesting the program cost $100 to $200 per net student going to college. For low-income students, the intervention led to an 8–12% increase in college enrollment. Ben and Lindsay tracked the students for several semesters and found they were more likely to stay enrolled in college than those who didn't get the proactive counseling.

Encouraged by the results they were seeing, Ben and Lindsay contacted more schools and thought about other ways to help students succeed. They designed lighter-touch interventions, such as text reminders, and partnered with schools across the country, as described in their book *Summer Melt: Supporting Low-Income Students through the Transition to College*.

Ben is now a faculty member at the University of Virginia, and Lindsay is a faculty member at the University of Pittsburgh; both are leaders in the emerging field of behavioral education interventions. Ben started an initiative called the Nudge4 Solutions Lab at UVA dedicated to behavioral economics and advised Michelle Obama's Reach Higher initiative. Lindsay has written for audiences ranging from practitioners and families to statisticians. Together, their work has made the US education system more inclusive and efficient.

Educational seat miles. Over at Harvard's policy school, Todd Rogers also began to think about behavioral education interventions.

Specifically, he decided to work on mobilizing and empowering students' social support systems to improve their achievement. He has now conducted interventions in over 2,000 schools and universities around the United States and Britain. His playbook looks a lot like his work on voting: finding low-cost, scalable interventions (think of versions of the Behavioural Insights Team's social norms letter, in which the team tweaked the tax letter to show what percentage of people had already paid their taxes), partnering with organizations to quantify the effect of the interventions, and then building an organization to scale their impact. Having established clear strategies for his work and raised significant funds, he has now started a small company aimed at implementing attendance nudges in schools and is well on his way to doing in education what he has already accomplished for voter behavior.

Todd has focused on a common problem that some schools have faced: high rates of student absenteeism. Over 10% of US K–12 students are chronically absent each year (defined as missing 18 or more days of school), with higher rates in low-income, urban districts.[1] Chronic absenteeism has been linked to lower academic performance, lower graduation rates, drug and alcohol use, criminality, and adverse outcomes later in life.[2]

Todd focuses on getting students into their seats. In one study, Todd and Avi Feller sent parents of 28,080 high-risk K–12 students one of three different sets of information throughout the school year. One group received no additional contact beyond normal school communications (e.g., report cards, school announcements, parent-teacher conferences). Parents in the second group received up to five rounds of mail throughout the school year reminding them of the importance of attendance and the ability of parents to influence attendance, along with information about their student's total number of absences that year. The third group received the same information as the second group, along with information about the students' absences in comparison to other students.

The results showed that for the two conditions in which parents received extra information, total absences were reduced by about 6% and chronic absenteeism by over 10% relative to the control group. Notably, given the chronic lack of funding in public education, these improvements were achieved at a low cost—$6 per additional day of student attendance. By comparison, paying and training absence-focused social workers and mentors to improve attendance can cost $121–$500 per school day.[3]

Interestingly, and contrary to Rogers and Feller's predictions, adding the social comparison information to the letters parents received did not further reduce student absences. For advocates of using social comparison or social norms to improve behavior, this might be a disappointment. We view it as an endorsement of the need to continually test results in new domains rather than simply assuming that an idea from laboratory research or other field settings will apply from one domain to the next. Sometimes we have a theory for why something should work in some areas but not others. In this case, the result came as a surprise even to the authors and spurred them to study it further. Based on their subsequent work, they believe that comparing students to unattainably better peers can be discouraging (e.g., "your child has missed 20 days of school and their comparison classmate has missed only 4 days"), whereas comparing students to attainably better peers can be motivating (e.g., "your child has missed 20 days of school and their comparison classmate has missed 18 days").[4]

Another lesson from this work is the prevalence of unintended consequences as companies and policymakers innovate. As it turned out, some parents complained about the letters, which they said made them feel worse about their child's attendance record in cases when the poor attendance was driven by serious illness or injury (think cancer or a broken bone). This prompted Todd and his collaborators to develop tools to better identify and exclude these families from receiving interventions like these, and better processes for addressing parent concerns when they arise. Refinements of this kind have been critical as they have begun to implement their interventions in school districts around the country. Experiments allow you to surface such issues before scaling up interventions, figuring out which aspects of innovations are effective, which can backfire, and which have unintended consequences.

In a related study, Todd worked with Carly Robinson, Monica Lee, and Eric Dearing in an attendance effort focused on K–5 students, on the hypothesis that habits developed at this early age are particularly important. They ran a randomized field experiment in ten school districts in California on 10,967 students, all of whom were in the bottom 60th percentile of attendance. The households in the control group (N = 4,388) received no additional communications beyond what is typically administered by their schools. A second group, "Mailing Only," also received mailings that emphasized the importance of regular school attendance during the earlier grades and provided information on the total number of days a student had been absent. Households in the third condition, "Mailing + Supporter," received the same information as in the second condition, plus supplementary inserts that encouraged parents to reach out to their "attendance supporters," a group that included relatives, friends, and other community/school members who support parents with attendance-related issues.

The two conditions that emphasized the importance of attendance and provided data on students' attendance were correlated with better attendance—0.53 fewer days missed—over the course of the school year, a 7.7% reduction in absences compared to students in the control condition, as well as a 14.9% reduction in chronic absenteeism. The cost of this intervention was $10.69 per each additional day of attendance generated. To their surprise, the extra social supporter information provided in the third condition did not statistically improve attendance over the second condition—a finding that shows how experiments can protect us from following our flawed intuitions down the wrong path.[5]

Using similar experimental communication strategies, but switching from mailing to the more efficient use of text messages, Peter Bergman and Eric Chan of Columbia University found that sending parents information about absences, missed assignments, and low student performance as they occur strongly improves attendance.[6] And Bergman and Rogers show that automatically enrolling families in such a program on an opt-out basis achieves much better results than an opt-in program that requires them to sign up.[7]

Overall, this work highlights an important use of experiments: they can fine-tune general frameworks. For example, long before Todd's social norms intervention, we knew from previous research that social norms *can* have an effect. But that doesn't mean that they *will* have an effect in every possible setting, nor tell us how to effectively communicate them. And it certainly doesn't tell us *how much* social norms will matter in that context, nor how to optimally implement them. Experiments allowed Todd and his collaborators to see that social comparisons (at least as they had been implementing them) seemed to be an ineffective strategy in their setting, which freed them to think about other potential interventions.

Experiments can help schools know whether and how to use social norms in their context, taking into account both the intended and unintended consequences. Faced with more possible messages than they can send to everyone, it helps them to know which will be most effective. This is clearly important to the mission of many schools, while falling outside of the off-the-shelf research that schools would otherwise rely on.

Grit. After a short career in consulting, Angela Duckworth became a seventh grade math teacher. She soon noticed that the most successful students weren't always the smartest (based on I.Q.); some of them were simply more persistent. Duckworth went on to graduate school and a faculty position at the University of Pennsylvania, where she developed the concept of grit, which she defines as "a combination of passion and perseverance for a singularly important goal," specifically for very long-term goals.[8]

In some contexts, Duckworth found that grit can help to predict success above and beyond traditional measures of intelligence. It was the predictive power of grit that brought it (and Duckworth) to fame. A group of educational reformers quickly became inspired by the idea. In particular, they were inspired by the notion that while grit may be measurable, it is also malleable, meaning that training efforts could be devised to improve students' grit and increase their success as a result. They seized on grit as a quality that can be fostered in children. Duckworth also became a central player in the move toward using comparatively low-cost field experiments to make beneficial societal changes. In this respect, her work mirrored the approach we've seen in other realms: use experiments to help figure out how and where interventions might be effective.

Among academics and policymakers in the education world, there has been a constant push-pull between the belief that individuals have relatively fixed traits (such as intelligence or grit) and the belief that many concepts that seem like traits are skills that can be developed. This struggle also is present in psychology between personality psychologists, who often seek to measure what they expect are fairly stable personality characteristics, and social psychologists, who have shown that situation often has a far greater influence on people than we would expect. This insight is central to the repeated discovery in the behavioral insights world that small changes to a person's environment can create surprisingly large changes in behavior. Duckworth and educational reformers are betting on the idea that grit can be taught, and some initial evidence supports this belief.

Notably, however, instilling grit in children doesn't entail just one simple intervention. It involves adopting a so-called "growth mindset" as well as "motivated deliberate practice." Psychologist Carol Dweck pioneered the concept of a growth mindset by showing that believing that basic abilities can be developed through dedication and hard work creates a joy of learning and a resilience that improves performance. In a 2016 study motivated by Dweck's work, David Yeager and his team developed a procedure to train ninth graders to have a more growth-oriented mindset. The three-stage mindset intervention began with having participants read a short scientific article entitled "You Can Grow Your Intelligence," which argued the brain can get smarter the more it is challenged. Next, students were asked to write about an example from their own lives of learning and getting smarter. Finally, they were asked to write an encouraging letter to a future student who might be struggling in school. The results showed that this fairly minimal intervention improved student GPA (in the year of the intervention) by .13 on a 0–4.33 scale (in a system that allowed for extra points for an A+).[9]

Another research team, led by Lauren Eskreis-Winkler and including Duckworth, developed a training module for sixth and seventh graders that taught the tenets of "deliberate practice": focus on your weaknesses, get feedback, concentrate, and repeat until mastery. Across multiple field experiments with training that lasted 25 or 50 minutes, the research team generally increased students' average GPA across a semester by about .1, with slightly larger increases for lower-performing students.[10]

A .1 change on a 0–4.0 (or 4.33) scale may not seem like a huge improvement, and in fact it isn't. But it is an impressive gain given that the result was replicated across multiple studies and the cost and amount of time spent on the intervention were so small. More broadly, there is good reason to think that the changes that Castleman, Page, Rogers, Duckworth, and others have achieved in the education realm might be more cost-effective than some of the costlier practices that have permeated educational policy—practices that largely were not tested with rigorous field experiments. Like the previous results, this work allowed schools to understand not just whether grit matters, but how to instill it in students.

These experiments have been part of the broader rise of randomized controlled trials in education. In recent years, there has been an increasing appreciation of the value of experiments in the world of education, including interest from funders, schools, and nonprofits in the use of experiments to directly test new ideas and inform decisions.

Wealthy

In 13 BCE, Rome's emperor Augustus feared that if retired soldiers were impoverished, they might revolt.[11] Augustus's solution was to assess new taxes to pay for a retirement benefit for soldiers. After serving at least 16 years in the military and four additional years in the reserves, soldiers would receive a one-shot payment of 3,000 denarii, which was about 13 times a soldier's yearly salary. This idea of receiving a defined benefit in return for many years of service has become a common form of retirement planning, known as defined benefit retirement accounts. In fact, by 1974, over two-thirds of all retirement funds were in defined benefit plans.[12] Of course, the concept has changed a great deal over 2,000 years, and the most common contemporary defined benefit plans pay a guaranteed amount per month or year for the life of the employee; but the focus on defining the benefit was maintained.

It is easy to see the appeal of defined benefit plans: The employer (or government) takes care of an employee's investment decisions, and the employee receives a guaranteed payout. The risk that the person will lead a long (and thus costly) life falls on the employer or government. In recent decades, a significant proportion of retirement plans have been moved instead toward defined contributions—that is, the firm's contribution to a retirement plan is fixed, and the opportunity (or burden) to make investments shifts to the employee.

Defined contribution plans often require active, voluntary participation by the employee. In some cases, the employer matches some amount of the employee's contributions. Even when match terms are very generous, employees often do not sign up, neglecting a great deal from their employer.[13] One culprit in the failure to save for retirement, as well as in the health behaviors discussed in the next section of this chapter, is what psychologists have termed present bias—the tendency for people to overweight current costs and benefits at the expense of what will happen to them in the future. Another culprit is that even people who mean to sign up might not get around to it, simply because they forget. More broadly, many would agree that it would be a good thing to encourage people to save more.

Based on these observations, considerable energy has been focused on finding ways to use behavioral insights to increase savings rates. In an influential 2003 paper, Esther Duflo and Emmanuel Saez teamed up with a university to run an experiment designed to encourage people to sign up for a tax-deferred retirement plan. In the experiment, they invited a sample of employees within some departments to attend a benefits information fair, offering payment for attendance. The incentive was effective in increasing attendance among those who were encouraged to attend. Perhaps more interestingly, the information spread. Not only were people who were offered payment more likely to attend the information sessions, but their colleagues were also more likely to attend. And the information provided at the sessions ultimately led to higher enrollment rates.[14]

A related approach was proposed by Annamaria Lusardi, an economist at the George Washington University, and her colleagues. The team provided new employees with an easy-to-follow, one-page planning guide for enrolling in a retirement savings plan, and found that people were 67% more likely to enroll as a response.[15]

While these strategies rely on providing information to employees, Brigitte Madrian and Dennis Shea suggested an even simpler strategy: changing the default on participating in a retirement plan. As we mentioned in chapter 3, they found that changing the status quo in a retirement savings plan dramatically increased people's savings. Examining the longer-term effects of this intervention at the same company and two others that followed very similar plans, James Choi and his colleagues found that after four years, 28% more employees were participating in the retirement plan compared to a system where they needed to opt in.[16]

Yet another approach to increasing retirement savings was proposed in Richard Thaler and Shlomo Benartzi's "Save More Tomorrow" plan, in which employees can commit in advance to increase their retirement savings rates as their pay increases.[17] The idea was that the temptation not to save would be less if you are making a choice about how much to save later rather than now. Benartzi and his colleagues have found that if participating in the plan is the default, the participation rate for "saving more tomorrow" is 83%—dramatically higher than the 27% participation rate when employees are required to opt in.[18]

These and other interventions have explored myriad ways to encourage retirement savings, which has rightfully been seen as an area in which behavioral experiments might leave people better off. But researchers have also been turning their attention to other—often more complicated—challenges around financial decision making, such as payday lending.

Payday lenders often charge shockingly high interest rates, ostensibly for a short amount of time. People often end up not being able to pay the loan back in time, which forces them to continue paying extremely high rates of interest. In one experiment, University of Chicago economists Marianne Bertrand and Adair Morse found that borrowers tend to overestimate the likelihood that they will be able to pay off the loan on their next payday. Partnering with a large payday loan company with many branches, they set out to see whether they could help to discourage people from borrowing money they wouldn't be able to pay back. With this goal in mind, they showed a subset of potential borrowers a simple infographic on the actual repayment rates of people like them. They found that even a simple information intervention reduced payday loan take-up by about 11% relative to the control group over the four months following the intervention.[19]

Of course, not all interventions have been successful (which is part of why it is important to experiment). In a large-scale randomized control experiment on financial education, conducted by Mariam Bruhn and her colleagues at the World Bank, 892 high schools agreed to have one of their classrooms participate in a 17-month financial education program. Between 72 and 144 hours of class time were devoted to the program, which included exercises for students to complete at home with their parents. This extensive treatment increased students' performance on a financial literacy exam and their overall grades at school, and improved their ability to get a job. In addition, the parents of students in the treatment condition on average scored higher on financial literacy and were more likely to save. However, the students who participated also engaged in more installment plan and credit card borrowing—suggesting they have been accruing debt as well.[20] This points to the complexity involved in understanding whether an intervention works. Had the team only seen the first few data points, they would have thought the intervention was an unambiguous success. It was only because they carefully tracked credit card borrowing and loans as well that they could see the full picture.

In a more unusual approach to financial education, two other World Bank development economists, Gunhild Berg and Bilal Zia, provided randomly selected South Africans with a financial incentive to watch a soap opera where messages about gambling and debt management were part of the storyline. Viewers of the soap opera, on average, scored higher on financial literacy and were more likely to borrow from lower-priced (as compared to higher-priced) formal creditors.[21]

Stepping back, there are similarities between the education and finance interventions reviewed here. As in the education case, experiments have helped researchers to understand which general frameworks are relevant in the financial decision-making context, and how to create a toolkit that makes sense for the problem at hand. In recent years, banks ranging from BPI in France to Commonwealth Bank of Australia have begun running their own experiments to further understand financial decision making.

... and Healthy

We've seen that a bias toward the present can keep people from making sound financial decisions for the future. Present bias also holds people back from being as healthy as they could be. Many of us would rather watch television than exercise, order French fries rather than salad—actions that undervalue the long-term implications of our actions. Similarly, Americans' failure to take their medicines as directed leads to an estimated $100 billion in hospital costs each year.[22] The short-term financial costs of the drugs, as well as their short-term side effects, stand in the way of smart long-term decision making, as does the simple problem of forgetfulness. Simple solutions are available, such as low-cost electronic reminders, yet many of these have not been implemented.[23]

Over the past decade, psychologists and behavioral economists have been exploring strategies to encourage healthier lifestyles. One of the world leaders in behavioral health is Kevin Volpp, a doctor and behavioral economist at the University of Pennsylvania. In one study, Kevin and his colleagues enrolled people who had been prescribed medication into a special lottery. If they took their meds, they had a low probability of winning a large reward. Those who failed to take their meds and won the lottery would not receive the prize—but they would learn that they were not going to earn the reward because of their failure to do what they were supposed to do. Volpp's experimental evidence shows that the lottery motivates people to take their medication.[24] In another study of his, a lottery also increased weight loss among those who were dieting. Volpp's research frequently draws on his deep understanding of cognitive biases, which he harnesses to help people make better decisions.[25] This intervention is based on empirical research suggesting that we tend to believe low-probability events are more likely than they actually are. Consequently, people spend too much money on lottery tickets, in part because they overweight the likelihood that they will win. Volpp was able to transform this attraction to lotteries into a positive in the realm of health. In addition, as described earlier, we also tend to weight losses more heavily than gains—a phenomenon known as loss aversion. Thus, people are motivated to take their meds to avoid the unpleasant feeling of finding out that they can't collect lottery winnings.

Another potential strategy documented through experimentation is what Wharton professor Katherine Milkman refers to as "temptation bundling." In her experiment, participants could only listen to a desirable audiobook when exercising at the gym—a loaner iPod was made available to them only at the gym, and they could pick which tempting audiobook to listen to while at the gym. Participants were much more likely to keep coming back to the gym when they knew a good book was waiting for them, Milkman found.[26]

In other research, Milkman and her colleagues adapted Todd Rogers's work on getting out the vote to increase vaccination rates. Having people think about and write down when they planned to get a vaccine increased the likelihood that they would actually follow through. Here again, plan making proved to be a successful, low-cost intervention.[27]

When selecting nudges to administer, it is also useful to consider which intervention will be easiest to maintain over time. One of the reasons that defaulting people into a retirement savings plan is so effective is that once they are in, the status quo bias leads them to stay enrolled. Interestingly, John Beshears and his colleagues—researchers who have worked primarily in the realm of financial nudges—have shown that a strong health benefit can be obtained by defaulting people into a home delivery drug program. These programs, which tend to be cheaper than picking up drugs at the pharmacy, increase the likelihood that patients will follow through on taking their meds.[28] The default sets up good habits.

This highlights an important lesson for experimentalists as well—which is to think carefully about the length of time you want to track an outcome for, which depends on the question at hand, and on the relationship between short-term and long-term outcomes. In our view, experiments can run the risk of focusing too much on the short run, in ways that can be harmful in the longer term. As we'll see in the next chapter, many behavioral interventions that have been shown to have a short-term effect are much less successful at leading to longer-term behavioral change.

13

The Behavior Change for Good Project

University of Pennsylvania professors Katherine Milkman and Angela Duckworth, whom you met in earlier chapters, like to walk to work together.[1] Katy is a professor in the Wharton business school, and Angela is in the psychology department. Their walk—a twenty-five-minute jaunt from their homes in Center City Philadelphia to campus—gives them time to catch up on life and research. Some days, they discuss the Philadelphia restaurant scene. Other days, they discuss experiments they are running that are aimed at improving the world around them.

In the summer of 2016, Katy and Angela spent a lot of time discussing an incredible opportunity that had crossed their desks. The MacArthur Foundation had just released a call for proposals for 100&Change, a $100 million award for a promising solution to a major societal challenge. Penn administrators quickly announced they would put forward only one proposal from the university. Could Katy and Angela leverage the growing enthusiasm for behavioral science and the strength of their own networks to win the prize?

Though they thought their chances of beating out hundreds of other contenders from around the world were slim, Katy and Angela agreed, "Let's do it anyway." Their proposed initiative, which they named Behavior Change for Good (BCFG), would unite social scientists and practitioners to create positive, durable behavior change in the realm of health, education, and savings. They defined "durable" to mean behavior change that persists for at least one year following the intervention.

The idea underlying BCFG was simple. People know they should be investing in their own education, exercise, and retirement. But as we saw in chapter 12, our best intentions can easily be derailed by short-run temptations—skipping class to sleep in, watching Netflix instead of going to the gym, or investing in chai lattes instead of a 401k. Ultimately, millions of Americans suffer—and even die—as a result of shortsighted decision making. Katy and Angela wanted to work with organizations and other researchers to identify effective ways to nudge people to make better decisions, and specifically to *change their habits over time.*

If the idea was simple, the project was extraordinarily complex. Joining a growing movement of practitioners and researchers, they sought to launch a multiyear series of dozens of simultaneous field experiments in each domain—health, education, and savings. Like the experiments of other applied research groups that you read about in earlier chapters, Katy and Angela's experiments would rely on and build upon several decades of work in the field of behavioral science. Compared to organizations like BIT and Ideas42, BCFG would focus on projects that would lead to academic research, which would ultimately help to guide the decisions Katy and Angela would make about which interventions to develop into actual experiments.

Katy and Angela

Before we tell you more about BCFG and how the project unfolded, we think you should know a little more about Katy and Angela. After graduating from Princeton, Katy entered a quirky joint PhD program at Harvard between the computer science department and the business school, where Max was her advisor. Katy's research on judgment and decision making was influenced by her personal experiences. Reflecting on some of her own "life hacks" for eating well, exercising, and saving money got her thinking about all of the temptations that made it hard to make good decisions, as well as the strategies that could enhance self-control and long-term decision making.

Katy began looking at situations in which people were conflicted between what they felt they *should* be doing (like going to the gym) and what they *want* to do in the short term (like ordering pizza). Looking at mail order DVD rentals (in a project with Max and Todd Rogers, whom we heard about last chapter), she found that when people order highbrow movies (movies they feel they *should* watch), they take much longer to return them relative to when they order lowbrow movies (movies they *want* to watch).[2] Studying grocery shopping, she found that small windfalls, like a $10-off coupon, caused people to splurge on items they wouldn't normally purchase rather than "banking" the savings for a future shopping trip.[3] This line of research got her thinking about how to get people to focus more on long-term decision making. As a tenured professor at the Wharton School at the University of Pennsylvania, where she holds a secondary appointment at Penn's medical school, Katy has studied topics ranging from the uptake of flu vaccines[4] to participation in retirement savings programs,[5] focusing largely on identifying ways to help people commit to making better decisions.

As for Angela, you read about her pioneering research on grit in the previous chapter. She received a MacArthur "genius grant" in 2013 for her research on grit and published a bestselling book on the topic. Her TED talk on the topic has been watched by over 13 million people.

"If we can figure out the science of behavior and behavior change, if we can figure out what is motivation and how to motivate people, what is frustration and how do we manage it, what is temptation and why do people succumb to it—that to me would be akin to the semiconductor," says Angela, who is the Christopher H. Browne Distinguished Professor of Psychology professor at the University of Pennsylvania, with secondary appointments at the schools of business and education.[6]

As you can see, Katy and Angela have approached the question of how to get people to make better long-term decisions from different angles. But they have a shared passion for finding answers to this question—and it is this drive that led them to collaborate on BCFG.

Ambitious Goals

Katy and Angela knew there was no single researcher who had the expertise needed to move the needle on health, education, and savings; nor was there one obvious corporate partner that could reach study participants interested in improving all of these aspects of their lives. So they conceived of the BCFG as a central convener and coordinator of organizations that could provide participants and researchers who wanted to test their ideas in the field. The project was bigger than anything Katy and Angela had undertaken before. It was also an idea they believed in deeply. "What if we could make meaningful progress on every major problem of the twenty-first century with a single solution?" Angela asked in a video promoting the project.[7]

To make this possible, Katy and Angela decided that they needed to accomplish three goals: develop ideas for behavioral interventions in collaboration with other researchers, identify a large set of potential study participants to test the interventions, and create a backbone organization that could coordinate the experiments.

While the Behavioural Insights Team was leading the charge on bringing behavioral experiments into practice, Katy and Angela saw an opportunity to create an organization more on the research side. The initiative would join a growing ecosystem of universities designing initiatives aimed at facilitating behavioral field experiments. In 2003, MIT had launched J-PAL (described in chapter 2), which now has more than 400 professionals across seven global offices and faculty affiliates from a variety of leading universities. J-PAL is dedicated to working with organizations to run experiments aimed at reducing poverty and improving wellbeing around the globe; it has now launched hundreds of experiments and transformed the landscape of economic development. More recently, Harvard created the Behavioral Insights Group (a group we are part of), a much lighter-touch initiative to informally connect 40 faculty members who use behavioral insights through field experiments for the public good. Harvard graduate students created a 700-member sister organization called the Behavioral Insights Student Group.

Through BCFG, Katy and Angela were providing an important addition to this landscape: they were offering researchers from many universities a platform to test their ideas on experimental participants in real-world organizations. Unlike existing initiatives, the organization was focused entirely on developing new behavior change research. Katy and Angela would collaborate on all of the projects launched through BCFG. The project promised to be a unique addition to the growing field-experiment ecosystem.

In health, they hoped to boost gym attendance, reduce smoking, improve medication adherence, get people walking, and encourage healthy supermarket purchases. In education, the initiative would focus on increasing class attendance and homework completion, and minimizing disciplinary incidents. In the realm of savings, they aimed to reduce spending and cash withdrawals, and increase savings. As the name suggests, the goal was to create positive changes that stick "for good"—which they defined as changes that would last at least one year.

From Dream to Reality

During their morning walks and then in their offices, Katy and Angela dreamed big as they put together their application for the 100&Change prize. "The possibility of a $100 million prize gave us license to call anyone," Katy recalled. She and Angela successfully recruited an A team of scientists across disciplines and universities, including Nobel laureates Jim Heckman and Richard Thaler; MacArthur "genius grant" award winners Colin Camerer and Sendhil Mullainathan; and *New York Times* bestselling authors Adam Grant, Robert Cialdini, and Carol Dweck. (We are currently both affiliated with the initiative as well.) Scientists said they were drawn to the project partly due to their admiration for Katy and Angela, partly because they were curious about BCFG's unique structure, and partly out of pure academic interest. These were the same interests that motivated Katy and Angela—but few had much time to devote to the day-to-day tasks of setting up and running a large-scale field experiment.

At the same time, Katy and Angela signed on 17 major public and private partners that were intrigued by the idea of collaborating with the best and brightest behavioral researchers. In health, they recruited 24 Hour Fitness, Blink Fitness, Humana, CVS Caremark, Weight Watchers, and Whole Foods. In education, KIPP, New York City Public Schools, Summit Public Schools, Philadelphia School District, and the College Board agreed to participate. In savings, leaders from Bank of America, HelloWallet (Morningstar), Acorns, and USAA expressed enthusiasm for running field trials with their customers.

To facilitate the deployment of the researchers' ideas in real organizations, Katy and Angela hired a small BCFG staff. An executive director and two research coordinators managed the many processes and relationships that make up BCFG, and a senior product manager and two application engineers built a web platform capable of deploying the interventions to hundreds of thousands of participants via email and text.

Katy and Angela were thrilled when Penn chose BCFG as the one proposal that it would advance to the MacArthur Foundation. Journalist Stephen Dubner, the host of the public radio show *Freakonomics Radio*, was fascinated by what Katy and Angela were up to and decided to follow the launch of their efforts.[8] Ultimately, the MacArthur Foundation did not select BCFG for the $100 million. However, the Penn administration, inspired by Katy and Angela's efforts and their prior successes, committed millions of dollars to the project.

Nudging to Improve Health

To show you how the BCFG process works, we'll concentrate on a project that Katy and Angela launched in the health domain with the primary goal of increasing people's participation in exercise. Their focus on increasing exercise was motivated by the growing literature on the malleability of Americans' exercise habits. Being paid to exercise for as little as one month had been shown to create lasting behavior change even after the incentives were removed.[9]

In addition, statistics suggested that Americans have lots of room to improve. Nearly half of American adults fail to meet the federal government's guidelines for aerobic physical activity.[10] When considering both aerobic activity and muscle-strengthening exercises, the failure rate increases to 88%. Yet Americans are aware they're not active enough, and they want to improve: 66% of Americans say they don't exercise enough, according to a national poll by Nielsen.[11]

In the long term, the failure to follow through on exercise plans can be deadly. Lack of physical activity is considered a contributing factor for developing heart disease, and it puts people at higher risk of stroke, type 2 diabetes, some cancers, arthritis, depression, and premature death.[12] The good news is that incrementally reducing Americans' physical inactivity can save lives. Researchers estimate that the 2.3% average nationwide decline in physical inactivity between 1980 and 2000 was associated with the acceleration of 17,445 deaths from coronary heart disease.[13]

In short, Katy and Angela knew improving exercise habits was possible, urgent, and in line with Americans' own intentions. To nudge people toward exercise, they approached two companies that have ready access to people interested in improving their health and to data on these customers' exercise habits: 24 Hour Fitness and Blink Fitness.

24 Hour Fitness is a national fitness club chain, reaching 3.7 million members across more than 420 locations in 13 states. When Angela emailed the company's CEO, Chris Roussos, about a possible partnership, he jumped at the opportunity, as he had been planning to assign her book, *Grit*, to his leadership team. Once they got talking, BCFG's potential benefits became clear to 24 Hour Fitness's leaders. Beyond the warm glow and favorable buzz that would come with the high-profile collaboration, the price was low (U Penn was covering the costs of the interventions) and it had the potential to help members of 24 Hour Fitness. Frank Napolitano, the company's president, believes that the company's growth is not only about selling memberships but engaging members. "[We have a] strong conviction that we want to get people to be active—to help them live longer, stronger, healthier lives," he said in an interview. "We want to get them involved."[14]

Additionally, 24 Hour Fitness points out that engaging members had the potential to help the company's bottom line. Though 24 Hour Fitness had long collaborated with researchers to develop fitness programming and to survey members, the large-scale experimentation and data-sharing inherent in the BCFG partnership would be unique in the company's 30-year history. The executives were excited about what could come from collaboration with some of the world's leading academic behavioral scientists.

Blink Fitness is New York-based value fitness club franchise reaching 250,000 members per year in more than 60 locations across four states.[15] Blink offers low monthly membership fees in exchange for access to the basics: fitness equipment and locker rooms. Blink is adamant that it is not in the business of signing up members its staff will never see. "We want to make quality fitness accessible," Blink Marketing VP Ellen Roggemann said in an interview.[16] When Katy and Angela approached Blink Fitness, its executives were excited about the possibility of understanding more about their members, encouraging exercise both inside and outside the gym, and exploring potential benefits to their brand.

The BCFG Launch

In May 2017, Katy and Angela convened the first meeting of BCFG team scientists at the University of Pennsylvania. The multiday workshop introduced the scientists to each other, and Katy and Angela previewed StepUp, the web-based platform their developers had created to host the interventions that the scientists were designing to increase participation in exercise.[17] It was only at this point that most members of the team of scientists began to fully appreciate the scope of—and effort involved in—Katy and Angela's plans for BCFG.

The StepUp program works on both computers and smartphones, and engages participants for 28 days. Gym members would visit the StepUp website to register, and the rest was up to the scientists. Using the StepUp platform, they could test promising ideas that borrow from and build on literature about what motivates people to work out. They could add content and questions to the registration process, and customize emails and texts that participants would receive. The BCFG team (Katy, Angela, and their team) tracked all interventions to manage which interventions would be implemented and how many users would be in each.

A month after the initial meeting, Katy and Angela sent a follow-up email to the team of scientists. The first round of experiments with 24 Hour Fitness and Blink Fitness would begin soon, they wrote. Now it was time for scientists to share ideas for specific interventions that would nudge fitness club members to exercise, using emails and text messages. The interventions should be simple, scalable, and manageable through StepUp, Katy and Angela explained. The BCFG team made the mechanics of running the studies simple. Now each scientist had a motivation to design an intervention that would be maximally effective.

Before reading further, having read most of this book, take a moment to think about what you would have proposed as an effective intervention.

While many of the experiments had some immediate benefit, the preliminary results suggest that some of the behavioral interventions that led to short-term gains were less effective when looked at over a multiple-month span—an important insight in a field that is often focused on short-term outcomes. This is also an important point for experimentalists: short-term outcomes can be misleading, and it can be valuable to invest in tracking data for a longer period. In the context of BCFG, we expect that this insight will help guide research toward interventions that will have longer-term effects—which is exactly the point of BCFG. (Although we finished this book before the results of this set of experiments were fully analyzed; you can visit https://bcfg.wharton.upenn.edu/ to find out more details.) In the words of Angela, "Behavior changes are really *#$@ing hard."

BCFG points to two additional important lessons for experimentalists. First, Katy and Angela's use of experiments was quite different from the approach used in Todd's education and voting experiments. They went out of their way to focus on interventions that were novel, even if this meant they were less likely to have any effect at all. The purpose of their experiments was to develop new academic frameworks. In contrast, Todd's earlier voting experiments were less concerned with novelty per se than on refining known frameworks and demonstrating the potential of the Analyst Institute to potential customers. These different uses of experiments are all perfectly legitimate.

A second lesson to emerge from BCFG is that the design of experiments depends on the incentives of the organization. If 24 Hour Fitness was to run its own experiments, it would likely focus less on academic novelty and more on maximizing impact for its customers—which, of course, is the company's goal. One might wonder why, then, a company would join such a collaboration. But there are good reasons for a company to do so, even if, by itself, it would have chosen different interventions and had different goals. After all, working with BCFG provided an influx of new ideas. Plus, the researchers and their funders bore the costs of developing the app and running the experiments—which is what allowed BCFG to focus on the research questions that most interested them, as opposed to the ones that would be most useful to the company involved. As a result, it's easy to see why the collaboration was a good deal for all parties involved, and is sure to provide useful insight for the world.

14

The Ethics of Experimentation

Experimentation has faced a significant amount of backlash over the years. When working with different governments on consulting, teaching, and research projects, we have run up against culture-specific norms that impede the use of experiments even when the stated goal is to help citizens make better decisions. For example, while working with different agencies of the Dutch government, we often heard that treating experimental participants in different conditions differently was at odds with a strong Dutch cultural norm of treating everyone the same. We try to be respectful of different cultural norms, but we believe aversion to experiments on the basis of unequal treatment can be misguided for two reasons.

First, we see experimentation as a form of learning. By experimenting, you can learn more and improve a product, policy, or a medical treatment in the long term. You might have a guess as to which condition is going to end up better off. And it's sad that some people will be given a treatment that you think might be worse. But, in the long run, this allows you to know with greater certainty which treatment is best, and to provide better care, products, and policies to the greatest number of people over the longer term. When deciding whether an experiment is ethical, we find it helpful to weigh these long-term benefits against short-term opportunity costs.

Experimentation When Incentives Are Not Aligned

Concerns about unequal treatment can occur even in situations where the experiment is aimed at learning something that will serve the greater good. However, a second set of concerns pertains to organizations using experiments to achieve goals less aligned with the social good. For example, most companies run experiments to make decisions aimed at increasing profits. Like many choices aimed at increasing profit, this can be good for customers but might not be. If your goal is to design the best possible product or service, experiments can help you do so more effectively. Just as we hope that leaders of for-profit organizations get their accounting right and communicate well, we also hope they will carefully vet their new ideas with experiments.

Yet companies do sometimes conduct experiments to figure out how to get consumers to pony up every last penny, improving the profitability of the firm — irrespective of the implications for customers. Running experiments focused on making an organization better off at the expense of consumers raises ethical questions and practical tradeoffs that managers need to think about. Is it OK to use experiments that may increase profit but leave your customers worse off? This question is certainly not unique to experiments, but experiments provide a unique opportunity for managers to be explicit about their goals, and about the tradeoffs they are and aren't willing to make. And, in our experience, this can also help managers to raise and address concerns that they otherwise would have swept under the rug.

Experiment Aversion

Another concern is what we call "experiment aversion"—people's fear of being guinea pigs in organizations' experiments. In our discussions, we have come across people who have an instinctive aversion to experiments even while they are accepting of organizations trying new ideas, thinking systematically about what to try and how to try it, trying new ideas on relatively small numbers of people rather than rolling out the idea without any testing, and looking at trial data systematically. Of course, when added together, these add up to the process of running experiments. Experimentation is simply a method for trying new ideas in a systematic manner.

Experiment aversion is not new. In his history of medical experimentation, Harry Marks quotes from US Veterans Administration documents from the 1940s: "We don't like to use the word 'experiments' in the Veterans Administration: 'investigation' or 'observations,' I believe is the approved term for such a study in the VA hospitals."[1] Similarly, the term A/B testing is often used euphemistically to describe experiments in companies. One tech company recently told us that they don't run experiments; they run "A/B tests." By having a better understanding of the value and risks of experiments, organizations can move beyond euphemisms and have more directed conversations about experiments—with the goal of learning while avoiding unnecessary risks.

The Moral Imperative to Experiment

The Behavioral Insights Group was created in 2013 within the Center for Public Leadership (CPL) at the Harvard Kennedy School of Government. Bringing the Behavioral Insights Group into the CPL raised questions about the nature of leadership. Previously, the CPL had not been closely connected to work of Kahneman, Tversky, and

Thaler, nor were experiments a common methodology for faculty connected to the Center.

During an early Behavioral Insights Group panel at the CPL, moderated by Max, a CPL faculty member spoke up to say that he found the presentations very interesting, but noted that leadership traditionally is aimed at changing the hearts and minds of followers. He was skeptical that experiments are part of the leadership toolkit.

This observation misses a key point: leaders are central to creating an organization dedicated to experimentation and evidence. David Halpern displayed leadership when he created the Behavioural Insights Team. Hal Varian displayed leadership when he pushed for experimentation within Google. And Angela Duckworth and Katy Milkman showed leadership when they made experimentation the central tenet of Behavior Change for Good. Good leaders have enough humility to admit what they don't know, identify the best options in an uncertain world, and experiment. They create organizations that learn and adapt, and experimentation is an important part of that process.

When we try out new ideas, why not do it in a manner that allows us to determine whether the change is actually effective? Failing to experiment wastes organizational resources and keeps us from learning from the strategies we try. It also raises ethical issues about ignoring evidence that would be easy to obtain.

15

A Final Case for Experiments and Some Concluding Lessons

So you've read this book, and maybe you're even ready to run an experiment. You ask Bill in accounting whether you can try tweaking a letter being sent to people whose payments are overdue. We would not be surprised if Bill still balks. Will it be complicated? Expensive? Unfair to customers or employees? Consequently, many managers (we're looking at you, Bill!) stick with the status quo, whether or not they have a good reason to do so. They're open to trying new ideas based on their intuition, but experimentation sounds scary.

As we've seen throughout the book, this reluctance is often unjustified. In fact, managers run beneficial experiments all the time without even realizing they are doing so. To see how these *incidental experiments* (a term coined by Mike and his collaborator Oliver Hauser) arise, consider the challenge that colleges face in matching students with roommates for their dorms. To facilitate the process, schools often begin by having students fill out a questionnaire to determine their preferences and generate a preferred set of matches. But the colleges then need to decide how to create pairings from a large set of suitable options.

There are a few ways they could go about this. One option would be to implement a market-based solution: auction off the "best" rooms in the "best" dorms, and let the chips fall where they may. Many schools shun this approach because it would create something that looks too much like a class system. Alternatively, schools could further interview students to try to determine their preferences and match them solely based on shared or complementary preferences, but such efforts can become complicated and costly. Instead, most schools usually implement a fair, simple, low-cost option: they *randomly* assign roommates (after the initial screening process).

As a result, some students with very active social lives are randomly matched with roommates who like a quiet room so they can work hard. Some roommates end up sharing similar demographic characteristics, while others end up with those who are very different from them. Academically inclined applicants may be matched with those who are more likely to struggle.

Note that these schools did not set out to run an experiment; they were simply trying to be fair by using random assignment for roommates. But in a world where roommates vary on definable characteristics, "random assignment" amounts to an experiment. The university may not have identified the variables on which students vary or studied the impact of these variables on the interesting outcomes, but it did conduct an *incidental experiment.*

The value of this random assignment was not lost on Bruce Sacerdote, a professor of economics who went to Dartmouth for his undergraduate degree before entering Harvard for his PhD in economics. Bruce didn't just attend Dartmouth—he now is a professor there, and has conducted academic research on the school. Bruce realized that he could use the random assignment to learn more about improving the college experience. Comparing similar students who were randomly assigned to different roommates at Dartmouth College, Bruce finds that students' roommates influenced their GPAs. Randomly assigned roommates also influenced one another's choice of social organizations: A student is 9% more likely to join a fraternity or sorority if their roommate does, for instance. Bruce used the school's Survey of Incoming Freshmen to further explore the nature of this influence. In the survey, incoming students were asked a battery of questions—such as how likely they thought they were to graduate with honors or join a fraternity— and, for each, were asked to respond "no chance," "very little chance," "some chance," or "a very good chance." When it came to grades, Bruce found that some students were more malleable to peer influence than others. Those who came to Dartmouth confident that they would graduate with honors—or confident that they would *not* graduate with honors—were less prone to peer influence on their grades than students who were less sure. When it came to Greek life, he saw a different story: students' responses to questions about whether they would ultimately join a fraternity or sorority were less predictive of their actual behavior. Moreover, their responses underpredicted the extent to which their decision would be influenced by their roommate.[1]

Incidental experiments like these happen all the time. Consider the National Spelling Bee, which started in 1925. Have you ever considered how the administrators of the spelling bee choose the order of the words presented to contestants? Perhaps obviously, random assignment seems like the fairest option, and is the choice of most spelling bees. Voilà—another incidental experiment! Analyzing data on the National Spelling Bee, Georgia State University economist Jonathan Smith showed that students are 13–64% more likely to make a mistake if the student who went before them answered a word correctly than if their predecessor answered incorrectly.[2] Even the best spellers fall prey to choking under pressure. (And every year around the time of the Bee, Jon now tweets his gripe about the issue.)

In organizations ranging from government offices to businesses, incidental experiments are common. The widespread use of lotteries to help allocate scarce resources is a prime example. For example, the Pakistani government uses a lottery to allocate a limited number of visas for citizens seeking to perform the Hajj pilgrimage to Mecca. Economists David Clingingsmith, Asim Khwaja, and Michael Kremer used the results of the lottery to understand how the Hajj affects those who perform the pilgrimage. They found that the pilgrimage led Hajjis, as compared to non-Hajjis, to increase their belief in peace and equality among ethnic groups, as well as their acceptance of female education and employment.[3] Similarly, Chicago Public Schools uses a lottery to decide which students will be admitted to different schools. Economists Julie Berry Cullen, Brian Jacob, and Steven Levitt used this variation between students to study the impact of going to better schools. They found that going to a better school didn't matter much in terms of traditional academic performance (at least among the schools they were looking at). However, the lottery winners ended up doing better than those who lost the lottery (and went to worse schools) on other dimensions; for example, they were less likely to be involved in disciplinary incidents or to be arrested.[4]

Once you start looking, you can't help noticing incidental experiments everywhere. Do you see any in your organization? If so, what insights might you glean from them?

The very existence of incidental experiments also helps to debunk the notion that experiments are inherently cumbersome beasts that should be avoided at all costs. It also becomes apparent that learning practical tasks that can reduce costs, creating a fair process for employees and customers, and increasing profits can align with the goal of seeking knowledge.

There's no reason to stop at incidental experiments. Intentional experiments can be an effective and low-cost way to learn. When you have a goal of learning what works, you can switch from running only incidental experiments to running more intentional ones as well, designing randomization in a way that best allows you to learn what works.

Experiments Are Part of the Leadership Toolkit

Throughout this book, we've seen the myriad ways in which experiments have begun to transform policy and business. We've seen their promise and power. Yet we've also seen that we're still in the early days of experiments in organizations. Effective experimentation requires managerial judgment, careful interpretation of results, and an appreciation of both the strengths and limitations of experiments.

Again and again, we've seen that leaders often rely on their very faulty intuition when making decisions about the future. As we mentioned in chapter 4, it was this recognition that helped to spawn the experimental revolution and gave rise to experiments in organizations. Simply put, leaders are responsible for making hard decisions—and experiments can help improve their decision making. Leaders need to have the humility and confidence to know what they don't know, and to use experiments as part of their toolkit for answering tough questions.

Leaders also have the power to influence whether others in their organization view experiments as a normal way to learn and adapt. It is not by chance that experiments are common in some organizations and foreign in others. Leaders set the tone, and those who are barriers to experimentation are also barriers to finding more effective ways for their organization to operate. Put differently, leaders are making a mistake if they think of experiments simply as a technical tool, disconnected from managerial decisions.

Looking at the experiments we've discussed in this book, we find important lessons for leaders, for those who run experiments, and for those making sense of the age of experiments. We've identified the following five overarching themes for those who want to leverage experiments in their organizations.

Theme 1: We are at the beginning of an experimental revolution. Throughout the book, we've seen experiments in areas ranging from tech to education to government. Over just a few short years, hundreds of teams dedicated to using behavioral insights have popped up in the public and private sectors, many of which have been bringing experiments to the forefront of decision making. Three core features have contributed to the rise of experiments. First, data has become ever more available, driven largely by the digitization of records and continued rise of online platforms. Second, online platforms have made randomization cheaper and easier. For tech companies, it's often standard operating procedure to have a hold-out group, and randomization often takes no more than the click of a button. Third, behavioral research has led to a greater appreciation of the large effects that even small changes can have on decisions and the extent to which human intuition can be flawed. Experiments can thus help to complement intuition with evidence.

Theme 2: Much of this has been good. Broadly speaking, using evidence to improve decisions is a positive development. This conclusion is not controversial. The British government tax letter described in chapter 1 was going out to delinquent taxpayers in any case; tinkering with it in an experiment allowed bureaucrats to find out which version of the letter would be most effective. In a variety of contexts, when policymakers or companies are thinking about how to most effectively allocate scarce resources, experiments can help them predict the returns on different options.

Theme 3: Because experimentation makes organizations smarter, they can have negative effects as well. Experiments help organizations learn and get better at achieving their goals. But what if you don't agree with those goals? In those cases, experiments are making organizations better at doing something you don't want them to do. In that sense, experiments are a tool—and like any tool, can be used for good or bad purposes.

Using experiments to help shroud fees may help make a company more effective at shrouding, but may leave customers worse off in the end.

Theme 4: Experiments are valuable well beyond the tech sector. As we have seen, the tech sector and governments were early adopters of experiments, but they are certainly not the only adopters. Experiments can be valuable well outside of technology and government. Leaders of for-profit and not-for-profit organizations and policymakers should think about when and where experiments might add value to their own organizations.

Theme 5: There is still a lot of work to be done. We are still in the early days of experimentation. As we've seen, experiments are commonplace in some contexts and undreamed-of in others. This is in part because experiments are simply better suited to some settings than to others. Yet it's also true that organizations are still trying to figure out how and when to use experiments. For example, experiments are central to decision making at Uber, but we know of at least one large ride-sharing company (outside of the United States) that doesn't run experiments at all—likely to their detriment. Even within organizations that run many experiments, experimentation can be challenging and unevenly applied. Even at Uber, they are still investing heavily in figuring out how to best run experiments and overcome the hurdles to drawing meaningful insights from them. Here at the start of the experimental revolution, there is much to be done, both in research and practice, to guide a more systematic approach to designing, evaluating, and making decisions based on experiments.

Using Experiments to Guide Organizational Decision Making

Throughout the book, we've seen experiments used in a variety of contexts with a variety of goals. Reflecting on them, we see four common ways that experiments are helping to improve decisions within organizations.

1. **Experiments can help evaluate an existing product or policy.** Sometimes organizations know exactly what they want to roll out. In these cases, an experiment can help measure the impact of the new policy or product and clarify both intended and unintended consequences. For example, Uber ran a series of experiments to evaluate its Express Pool product, in which Uber users can cut costs by walking to the nearest "Express" pick-up spot and ridesharing with other users. In many ways, this was a policy evaluation: Would the policy be an improvement, or not? Uber learned that, overall, Express Pool made users better off, though some simply switched from other products to Express Pool. And while this might make users better off, Uber would also like to know whether it makes Uber as a whole better off.

2. **Experiments can test a theory or hypothesis.** Even if you have a particular product or policy in mind, it's often helpful to understand *why* or *how* the policy is having an effect. In these cases, experiments can help to test a specific hypothesis. For example, in Airbnb's test of discrimination, the platform might want to understand whether a policy change reduces discrimination by correcting hosts' beliefs or simply by making race less salient. This difference can help to inform further product changes and generate a better understanding of why discrimination is so prevalent on the platform and how to reduce it. Mechanism experiments, which are designed to help

understand why a change is having an impact (rather than just that a change is having an impact) can help to test hypotheses.

3. **Experiments can help develop or refine frameworks.** Experiments can also help organizations develop frameworks to apply across decisions. The more frequently an organization encounters a certain type of decision, the more valuable having a framework (rather than simply a product evaluation) can become. As we saw in the Behavior Change For Good experiments in chapter 12 (in which Angela Duckworth and Katy Milkman ran experiments with 24 Hour Fitness and other organizations), the experiments allow for the creation of new academic theories where existing ones are insufficient, with the goal of generalizing to a variety of different settings. (Their goal was to develop theories of how psychology can help lead to long-term behavior change, which they defined as changing behavior for a year or more.) And as we saw in the education experiments Todd Rogers ran, he took off-the-shelf behavioral theories (like the social norms intervention that the Behavioural Insights Team popularized) and used experiments to understand whether and how schools could use them to increase attendance. In this case, experiments allowed organization to fine-tune existing theories to a particular context.

4. **Experiments can be used for fact finding where no theory yet exists.** As we've mentioned, sometimes you don't have a hypothesis. In these cases, experiments can still help with fact finding to help you get a sense of what might be missing from existing frameworks. As we mentioned before, eBay might not have a theory for whether its choice of font, or the gender of actors in its advertisements, affect product usage. But eBay leaders might care, and experiments can help them to figure out the answers.

Should Informed Citizens Be Experiment Averse?

Are you in favor of trying new ideas that seem like promising improvements on the status quo? When trying a new idea, would you like to think systematically about whether it will be an improvement or not? Would you like to make this assessment as objectively as possible? Would you like to minimize the cost of trying the new idea if it doesn't work?

It wouldn't be surprising if your answer to each of these questions was yes. If so, you are likely in favor of experimentation. Experiments are simply a way to systematically and objectively try new ideas. The better our experiments are run, the more accurate our evidence of the promise of a new idea will be. Thus, we believe that informed citizens should become fans of experimentation.

But to be in favor of experimentation, we also need to accept uncertainty—to understand that we might invest effort and end up concluding that a new idea is not effective. A well-designed experiment allows us to reach such an understanding at a relatively low cost. We believe that citizens should encourage government officials to admit when they don't know the answer to a policy question and to experiment to find out the answer. We should back politicians who are aware of "nudge units" and believe they can create more efficient government around the globe.

Put differently, experiments have great potential for good. But, as with all evidence gathering, the value of the evidence depends entirely on the people running the experiments. If an organization is using experiments to figure out how to bilk you, that's great for the company but not so much for you. We don't want to throw those worries away, but we are optimistic that with enough transparency and boundaries put on organizations, we can get the value of experiments while avoiding some of the worst abuses.

In 1933, composer and songwriter Cole Porter wrote the song "Experiment" for the musical *Nymph Errant*. While the musical had a different type of experimentation in mind, the conclusion was prescient—suggesting that we "do what all good scientists do. Experiment."

As this book comes to a close, the age of experiments is only beginning.

Notes

Acknowledgments

1 Chapter 1 of this book incorporates material from Michael Luca and Oliver Hauser, "Good Communication Requires Experimenting with Your Language," *Harvard Business Review*, February 4, 2016, https://hbr.org/2016/02/good-communication-requires-experimenting-with-your-language; chapter 15 incorporates material from Oliver Hauser and Michael Luca, "Your Company Is Full of Good Experiments (You Just Have to Recognize Them)," *Harvard Business Review*, November 23, 2015, https://hbr.org/2015/11/your-company-is-full-of-good-experiments-you-just-have-to-recognize-them. More generally, the Uber Express pool experiment is discussed in Jeff Fossett, Duncan Gilchrist, and Michael Luca, "Using Experiments to Launch New Products," *Harvard Business Review*, November 5, 2018, https://hbr.org/2018/11/using-experiments-to-launch-new-products; and the Facebook experiment is discussed in Michael Luca, "Were OkCupid's and Facebook's Experiments Unethical?," *Harvard Business Review*, July 29, 2014, https://hbr.org/2014/07/were-okcupids-and-facebooks-experiments-unethical.

Chapter 1

1 Michael Hallsworth, John A. List, Robert D. Metcalfe, and Ivo Vlaev, "The Behavioralist as Tax Collector: Using Natural Field Experiments

to Enhance Tax Compliance," *Journal of Public Economics* 148 (2017): 14–31.

2 Behavioural Insights Team, "EAST: Four Simple Ways to Apply Behavioural Insights," http://www.behaviouralinsights.co.uk/wp-content/uploads/2015/07/BIT-Publication-EAST_FA_WEB.pdf.

3 Some of the experiments are presented in Hallsworth et al., "The Behavioralist as Tax Collector."

4 *Holy Bible, Good News Translation*, 2nd ed. (New York: American Bible Society, 1992), Daniel 1:8.

5 Ibid., Daniel 1:13.

6 Ibid., Daniel 1:17.

7 Ibid., Daniel 1:20.

8 T. Ostbye and J. Rochon, "An Early 'Clinical Trial' as a Teaching Exercise: The Book of Daniel 1.1–15 (1.1–20)," *Medical Education* 27 (1993): 97–101.

9 John P. Bull, "A Study of the History and Principles of Clinical Therapeutic Trials," MD thesis, University of Cambridge, 1951.

10 Arun Bhatt, "Evolution of Clinical Research: A History before and beyond James Lind," *Perspectives in Clinical Research* 1, no. 1 (2010): 6–10.

11 James Lind, *Treatise on Scurvy* (Edinburgh, 1753).

12 Steven D. Levitt and John A. List, "Field Experiments in Economics: The Past, the Present, and the Future," *European Economic Review* 53, no. 1 (2009): 1–18.

13 Ibid.

14 National Institutes of Health, "Estimates of Funding for Various Research, Condition, and Disease Categories (RCDC)," *Research Portfolio Online Reporting Tools*, March 15, 2011, https://web.archive.org/web/20110813065343/http:/report.nih.gov/rcdc/categories/Default.aspx.

Chapter 2

1 Ludy T. Benjamin Jr., *A Brief History of Modern Psychology* (Malden, MA: Blackwell Publishing, 2007).

2 Thomas H. Leahey, *A History of Modern Psychology* (Englewood Cliffs, NJ: Prentice-Hall, 1991).

3 Benjamin, *A Brief History of Modern Psychology*.

4 John B. Watson, "Psychology as the Behaviorist Views It," *Psychological Review* 20 (1913): 158–177.

5 Stanley Milgram, *Obedience to Authority: An Experimental View* (New York: Harper Collins, 1974).

6 Gina Perry, *Behind the Shock Machine: The Untold Story of the Notorious Milgram Psychology Experiments* (New York: New Press, 2013); Joseph Dimow, "Resisting Authority: A Personal Account of the Milgram Obedience Experiments," *Jewish Currents* 15 (2004): 1–5.

7 For more information about the Stanford Prison Experiment, you can visit http://www.prisonexp.org/.

8 Kenneth B. Clark and Mamie P. Clark, "Racial Identification and Preference among Negro Children," in Eugene L. Hartley, ed., *Readings in Social Psychology* (New York: Holt, Rinehart, and Winston, 1947).

9 Anthony G. Greenwald, Debbie E. McGhee, and Jordan L. K. Schwartz, "Measuring Individual Differences in Implicit Cognition: The Implicit Association Test," *Journal of Personality and Social Psychology* 74, no. 6 (1998): 1464–1480.

10 Brian A. Nosek, Mahzarin R. Banaji, and Anthony G. Greenwald, "Harvesting Implicit Group Attitudes and Beliefs from a Demonstration Web Site," *Group Dynamics: Theory, Research, and Practice* 6, no. 1 (2002): 101–115.

11 Mahzarin R. Banaji, "Ordinary Prejudice," *Psychological Science Agenda, American Psychological Association* 14 (2001): 8–11.

12 Edward E. Leamer, "Let's Take the Con out of Econometrics," *American Economic Review* 73, no. 1 (1983): 31–43.

13 Heather Ross, "An Experimental Study of the Negative Income Tax," thesis, Massachusetts Institute of Technology, Department of Economics, 1970.

14 E. H. Chamberlin, "An Experimental Imperfect Market," *Journal of Political Economy* 56 (1948): 95–108.

15 Heinz Sauermann and Reinhard Selten, "Ein oligopolexperiment," *Zeitschrift für die gesamte Staatswissenschaft / Journal of Institutional and Theoretical Economics* 3 (1959): 427–471.

16 Merrill M. Flood, "Some Experimental Games," *Management Science* 5 (1959): 5–26; Lawrence E. Fouraker and Sidney Siegel, *Bargaining Behavior* (New York: McGraw Hill, 1963); G. K. Kalish, J. W. Milnor, J. Nash, and E. D. Nehrig, "Some Experimental n-Person Games," in R. M. Thrall, C. H. Coombs, and R. L. Davis, eds., *Decision Processes* (New York: Wiley, 1954); Sidney Siegel and Lawrence E. Fouraker, *Bargaining and Group Decision Making* (New York: McGraw Hill, 1960).

17 Vernon L. Smith, "Experimental Economics: Induced Value Theory," *American Economic Review* 66, no. 2 (1976): 274–279; Vernon L. Smith, "Microeconomic Systems as an Experimental Science," *American Economic Review* 72, no. 5 (1982): 923–955.

18 George Loewenstein, "Experimental Economics from the Vantage-Point of Behavioral Economics," *Economic Journal* 109, no. 453 (1999): S25–S34.

19 Colin Camerer, "Rules for Experimenting in Psychology and Economics, and Why They Differ," in W. Guth and E. Van Damme, eds., *Understanding Strategic Interaction: Essays in Honor of Reinhard Selten* (New York: Springer-Verlag, 1996).

20 Nobel Media AB 2018, "Alvin E. Roth—Biographical," *NobelPrize.org* (2018), https://www.nobelprize.org/prizes/economics/2012/roth/auto -biography/.

21 Ibid.

22 Amos Tversky and Daniel Kahneman, "The Framing of Decisions and the Psychology of Choice," *Science* 211 (January 30, 1981): 453–458.

23 Devin G. Pope and Maurice E. Schweitzer, "Is Tiger Woods Loss Averse? Persistent Bias in the Face of Experience, Competition, and High Stakes," *American Economic Review* 101, no. 1 (2011): 129–157.

24 Roland G. Fryer, Steven D. Levitt, John List, and Sally Sadoff, "Enhancing the Efficacy of Teacher Incentives through Loss Aversion: A Field Experiment," National Bureau of Economic Research Working Paper No. 18237, 2012.

25 Richard Thaler, "Toward a Positive Theory of Consumer Choice," *Journal of Economic Behavior and Organization* 1 (1980): 39–80.

26 Glenn W. Harrison and John A. List, "Field Experiments," *Journal of Economic Literature* 42, no. 4 (2004): 1009–1055.

27 Abhijit Banerjee, Esther Duflo, and Michael Kremer, "The Influence of Randomized Controlled Trials on Development Economics Research and on Development Policy," https://scholar.harvard.edu/files/kremer/ files/the-influence-of-rcts-on-developmental-economics-research-and -development-policy.pdf.

28 Paul Glewwe, Michael Kremer, and Sylvie Moulin, "Many Children Left Behind? Textbooks and Test Scores in Kenya," *American Economic Journal: Applied Economics* 1, no. 1 (2009): 112–135.

29 Michael Kremer, "Randomized Evaluations of Educational Programs in Developing Countries: Some Lessons," *American Economic Review* 93, no. 2 (2003): 102–106.

Chapter 3

1 Eric J. Johnson and Daniel G. Goldstein, "Do Defaults Save Lives?," *Science* 302 (2003): 1338–1339.

2 U.S. Department of Health and Human Services, Health Resources and Services Administration, "2012 National Survey of Organ Donation Attitudes and Behaviors," September 2013, https://www.organdonor .gov/sites/default/files/about-dot/files/nationalsurveyorgandonation .pdf.

3 Richard H. Thaler, "Opting In vs. Opting Out," *New York Times*, September 26, 2009.

4 Judd Kessler and Alvin Roth, "Don't Take No for an Answer: An Experiment with Actual Donor Registrations," working paper.

5 Julian J. Zlatev, David P. Daniels, Hajin Kim, and Margaret A. Neale, "Default Neglect in Attempts at Social Influence," *PNAS* 114, no. 52 (2017): 13643–13648, https://doi.org/10.1073/pnas.1712757114.

6 Interview with Al Roth, May 30, 2019.

7 Richard H. Thaler and Cass R. Sunstein, *Nudge: Improving Decisions about Health, Wealth, and Happiness* (New Haven: Yale University Press, 2008).

8 Cass R. Sunstein and Richard H. Thaler, "Libertarian Paternalism," *American Economic Review* 93, no. 2 (2003): 175–179.

9 Keith E. Stanovich and Richard F. West, "Individual Differences in Reasoning: Implications for the Rationality Debate," *Behavioral and Brain Sciences* 23 (2000): 645–665; Daniel Kahneman, "Mapping Bounded Rationality: A Perspective on Intuitive Judgment and Choice," Nobel Lecture, Stockholm, Sweden, December 8, 2002; Daniel Kahneman, *Thinking, Fast and Slow* (New York: Farrar, Strauss, Giroux, 2011).

10 William Samuelson and Richard J. Zeckhauser, "Status Quo Bias in Decision Making," *Journal of Risk and Uncertainty* 1 (1988): 7–59.

11 Steven D. Levitt and John A. List, "Viewpoint: On the Generalizability of Lab Behaviour to the Field," *Canadian Journal of Economics* 40, no. 2 (2007): 347–370; Steven D. Levitt and John A. List, "What Do Laboratory Experiments Measuring Social Preferences Reveal about the Real World?," *Journal of Economic Perspectives* 21, no. 2 (2007): 153–174.

Chapter 4

1 Joseph O. Eastlack Jr. and Ambar G. Rao, "Advertising Experiments at the Campbell Soup Company," *Marketing Science* 8, no. 1 (1989): 57–71.
2 Haniya Rae, "How Consumer Reports Tests Vacuums," August 8, 2018, https://www.consumerreports.org/vacuum-cleaners/how-consumer-reports-tests-vacuums/.
3 Raphael Lopez Kaufman, Jegar Pitchforth, and Lukas Vermeer, "Democratizing Online Controlled Experiments at Booking.com," 2017, presented at the 2017 Conference on Digital Experimentation (CODE@MIT), https://arxiv.org/abs/1710.08217.
4 Interview with Ron Kohavi.
5 Michael Ostrovsky and Michael Schwarz, "Reserve Prices in Internet Advertising Auctions: A Field Experiment," working paper, 2016.
6 Ron Kohavi and Stefan Thomke, "The Surprising Power of Online Experiments," *Harvard Business Review*, September-October 2017.
7 Ibid.

Chapter 5

1 Fiona Scott Morton, Florian Zettelmeyer, and Jorge Silva-Russo, "Customer Information and Discrimination: Does the Internet Affect the Pricing of New Cars to Women and Minorities?," *Quantitative Marketing and Economics* 1, no. 1 (2003): 65–92.
2 Interview with Reed Kennedy.
3 Benjamin Edelman and Michael Luca, "Digital Discrimination: The Case of Airbnb.com," 2014, working paper.
4 Marianne Bertrand and Sendhil Mullainathan, "Are Emily and Greg More Employable Than Lakisha and Jamal? A Field Experiment on Labor Market Discrimination," *American Economic Review* 94, no. 4 (2004): 991–1013.
5 Raymond Fisman and Michael Luca, "Fixing Discrimination in Online Marketplaces," *Harvard Business Review*, December 2016.
6 Laura W. Murphy, "Airbnb's Work to Fight Discrimination and Build Inclusion: A Report Submitted to Airbnb," September 8, 2016, https://blog.atairbnb.com/wp-content/uploads/2016/09/REPORT_Airbnbs-Work-to-Fight-Discrimination-and-Build-Inclusion.pdf.

Chapter 6

1 Daisy Dai and Michael Luca, "Effectiveness of Paid Search Advertising: Experimental Evidence," Harvard Business School NOM Unit Working Paper No. 17-025, 2016.

Chapter 7

1 Dennis Zhang, Hengchen Dai, Lingxiu Dong, Fangfang Qi, Nannan Zhang, Xiaofei Liu, and Jiang Yang, "How Do Price Promotions Affect Customer Behavior on Retailing Platforms? Evidence from a Large Randomized Experiment on Alibaba," *Management Science*, forthcoming.

Chapter 8

1 N. Gregory Mankiw, "I Paid $2,500 for a 'Hamilton' Ticket. I'm Happy About It," *New York Times*, October 21, 2016, https://www.nytimes .com/2016/10/23/upshot/i-paid-2500-for-a-hamilton-ticket-im-happy -about-it.html.
2 Thomas Blake, Sarah Moshary, Kane Sweeney, and Steve Tadelis, "Price Salience and Product Choice," working paper, 2017, https://www.dropbox .com/s/ikrtnk5nvcrryc2/BMST.pdf?dl=0.
3 Xavier Gabaix and David Laibson, "Shrouded Attributes, Consumer Myopia, and Information Suppression in Competitive Markets," *Quarterly Journal of Economics* 121, no. 2 (2006): 505–540.

Chapter 10

1 US Office of the Director of National Intelligence, "Assessing Russian Activities and Intentions in Recent U.S. Elections," CreateSpace Independent Publishing Platform, 2017.
2 Alex Peysakovich and Seth Stephens-Davidowitz, "How Not to Drown in Numbers," *New York Times*, May 2, 2015.
3 http://www.nbc.com/saturday-night-live/video/debbie-downer/ 3505987.

4 Adam D. I. Kramer, Jamie E. Guillory, and Jeffrey T. Hancock, "Experimental Evidence of Massive-Scale Emotional Contagion through Social Networks," *PNAS* 111, no. 24 (2014): 8788–8790.

5 Vindo Goel, "Facebook Tinkers With Users' Emotions in News Feed Experiment, Stirring Outcry," *New York Times*, June 29, 2014, https://www.nytimes.com/2014/06/30/technology/facebook-tinkers-with-users-emotions-in-news-feed-experiment-stirring-outcry.html.

6 https://en.wikipedia.org/wiki/Doge_(meme).

7 Aleecia M. McDonald and Lorrie Faith Cranor, "The Cost of Reading Privacy Policies," *I/S: A Journal of Law and Policy for the Information Society*, 2008 "Privacy Year in Review" issue, http://www.is-journal.org/.

8 https://research.fb.com/.

Chapter 11

1 Harold Gosnell, *Getting Out the Vote: An Experiment in the Stimulation of Voting* (Chicago: University of Chicago Press, 1927).

2 Donald P. Green and Alan S. Gerber, "Introduction to Social Pressure and Voting: New Experimental Evidence," *Political Behavior* 32, no. 3 (2010): 331–336.

3 Todd Rogers, Donald Green, John Ternovski, and Carolina Young, "Social Pressure and Voting: A Field Experiment Conducted in a High-Salience Election," *Electoral Studies* 46 (2017): 87–100.

Chapter 12

1 Robert Balfanz and Vaughan Byrnes, "The Importance of Being in School: A Report on Absenteeism in the Nation's Public Schools," Johns Hopkins University Center for Social Organization of Schools, 2012; Michael A. Gottfried, "Excused versus Unexcused: How Student Absences in Elementary School Affect Academic Achievement," *Educational Evaluation and Policy Analysis* 31, no. 4 (2009): 392–415.

2 Todd Rogers and Avi Feller, "Reducing Student Absences at Scale by Targeting Parents' Misbeliefs," *Nature Human Behaviour* 2, no. 5 (2018): 335–342.

3 Robert Balfanz and Vaughan Byrnes, "Meeting the Challenge of Combating Chronic Absenteeism: Impact of the NYC Mayor's Interagency

Task Force on Chronic Absenteeism and School Attendance and its Implications for Other Cities," Johns Hopkins School of Education, 2013; Jonathan Guryan, Sandra Christenson, Amy Claessens, Mimi Engel, Ijun Lai, Jens Ludwig, Ashley Cureton Turner, and Mary Clair Turner, "The Effect of Mentoring on School Attendance and Academic Outcomes: A Randomized Evaluation of the Check & Connect Program," Northwestern Institute for Policy Research Working Paper WP-16-18, 2017.

4 Rogers and Feller, "Reducing Student Absences at Scale by Targeting Parents' Misbeliefs."

5 Carly D. Robinson, Monica G. Lee, Eric Dearing, and Todd Rogers, "Reducing Student Absenteeism in the Early Grades by Targeting Parental Beliefs," *American Educational Research Journal* (2017), https://doi.org/10.3102/0002831218772274.

6 Peter Bergman and Eric Chan, "Leveraging Technology to Engage Parents at Scale: Evidence from a Randomized Controlled Trial," CESifo Working Paper Series No. 6493, 2017.

7 Peter Bergman and Todd Rogers, "Is This Technology Useless? How Seemingly Irrelevant Factors Affect Adoption and Efficacy," HKS Working Paper No. RWP17-021, 2017.

8 Angela L. Duckworth, Christopher Peterson, Michael D. Matthews, and Dennis R. Kelly, "Grit: Perseverance and Passion for Long-Term Goals," *Journal of Personality and Social Psychology* 92, no. 6 (2007): 1087.

9 David S. Yeager, Carissa Romero, Dave Paunesku, Christopher S. Hulleman, Barbara Schneider, Cintia Hinojosa, Hae Yeon Lee, et al., "Using Design Thinking to Improve Psychological Interventions: The Case of the Growth Mindset during the Transition to High School," *Journal of Educational Psychology* 108, no. 3 (2016): 374.

10 Lauren Eskreis-Winkler, Elizabeth P. Shulman, Victoria Young, Eli Tsukayama, Steven M. Brunwasser, and Angela L. Duckworth, "Using Wise Interventions to Motivate Deliberate Practice," *Journal of Personality and Social Psychology* 111, no. 5 (2016): 728.

11 James J. Choi, "Contributions to Defined Contribution Pension Plans," NBER Working Paper No. w21467, 2015.

12 Ibid.

13 John Beshears, James J. Choi, David Laibson, and Brigitte C. Madrian, "Behavioral Household Finance," in B. Douglas Bernheim, Stefano DellaVigna, and David Laibson, eds., *Handbook of Behavioral Economics: Foundations and Applications* (Amsterdam: Elsevier, forthcoming).

14 Esther Duflo and Emmanuel Saez, "The Role of Information and Social Interactions in Retirement Plan Decisions: Evidence from a Randomized Experiment," *Quarterly Journal of Economics* 118, no. 3 (2003): 815–842.

15 Annamaria Lusardi, Punam Keller, and Adam Keller, "New Ways to Make People Save," in Annamaria Lusardi, ed., *Overcoming the Saving Slump: How to Increase the Effectiveness of Financial Education and Saving Programs* (Chicago: University of Chicago Press, 2009).

16 James J. Choi, David Laibson, and Brigitte C. Madrian, "Plan Design and 401(k) Savings Outcomes," *National Tax Journal* 57 (2004): 275–298.

17 Richard H. Thaler and Shlomo Benartzi, "Save More Tomorrow™: Using Behavioral Economics to Increase Employee Saving," *Journal of Political Economy* 112, no. S1 (2004): S164–S187.

18 Shlomo Benartzi, Ehud Peleg, and Richard H. Thaler, "Choice Architecture and Retirement Saving Plans," in Eldar Shafir, ed., *The Behavioral Foundations of Public Policy* (Princeton, NJ: Princeton University Press, 2012).

19 Marianne Bertrand and Adair Morse, "Information Disclosure, Cognitive Biases, and Payday Borrowing," *Journal of Finance* 66, no. 6 (2011): 1865–1893.

20 Miriam Bruhn, Luciana de Souza Leão, Arianna Legovini, Rogelio Marchetti, and Bilal Zia, "The Impact of High School Financial Education: Experimental Evidence from Brazil," World Bank Policy Research Working Paper No. 6723, 2013.

21 Gunhild Berg and Bilal Zia, "Harnessing Emotional Connections to Improve Financial Decisions: Evaluating the Impact of Financial Education in Mainstream Media," *Journal of the European Economic Association* 15, no. 5 (2017), https://doi.org/10.1093/jeea/jvw021.

22 Regina M. Benjamin, "Medication Adherence: Helping Patients Take Their Medicines As Directed," *Public Health Reports* 127, no. 1 (2012): 2–3, doi: 10.1177/003335491212700102.

23 Marcia Vervloet, Annemiek J. Linn, Julia C. M. van Weert, Dinny H. De Bakker, Marcel L. Bouvy, and Liset Van Dijk, "The Effectiveness of Interventions Using Electronic Reminders to Improve Adherence to Chronic Medication: A Systematic Review of the Literature," *Journal of the American Medical Informatics Association* 19, no. 5 (2012): 696–704.

24 Kevin G. Volpp, George Loewenstein, Andrea B. Troxel, Jalpa Doshi, Maureen Price, Mitchell Laskin, and Stephen E. Kimmel, "A Test of

Financial Incentives to Improve Warfarin Adherence," *BMC Health Services Research* 8, no. 1 (2008): 272.

25 Kevin G. Volpp, Leslie K. John, Andrea B. Troxel, Laurie Norton, Jennifer Fassbender, and George Loewenstein, "Financial Incentive–Based Approaches for Weight Loss: A Randomized Trial," *JAMA* 300, no. 22 (2008): 2631–2637.

26 Katherine L. Milkman, Julia A. Minson, and Kevin G. M. Volpp, "Holding the Hunger Games Hostage at the Gym: An Evaluation of Temptation Bundling," *Management Science* 60, no. 2 (2013): 283–299.

27 Katherine L. Milkman, John Beshears, James J. Choi, David Laibson, and Brigitte C. Madrian, "Using Implementation Intentions Prompts to Enhance Influenza Vaccination Rates," *Proceedings of the National Academy of Sciences of the United States of America* 108, no. 26 (2011): 10415–10420.

28 John Beshears, James Choi, David Laibson, and Brigitte Madrian, "Active Choice and Health Care Costs: Evidence from Prescription Drug Home Delivery," working paper, 2012.

Chapter 13

1 This chapter is adapted from a forthcoming Harvard Business School case, "Behavioral Change For Good—A Case." The case was coauthored with Marie Lawrence, who contributed significantly to the content conveyed in this chapter. Max Bazerman is a Team Scientist on the Behavior Change For Good Initiative.

2 Katherine Milkman, Todd Rogers, and Max H. Bazerman, "Highbrow Films Gather Dust: Time-Inconsistent Preferences and Online DVD Rentals," *Management Science* 55, no. 6 (2009): 1047–1059.

3 Katherine Milkman and John Beshears, "Mental Accounting and Small Windfalls: Evidence from an Online Grocer," *Journal of Economic Behavior and Organization* 71 (2009): 384–394.

4 Katherine Milkman, John Beshears, James J. Choi, David Laibson, and Brigitte C. Madrian, "Using Implementation Intentions Prompts to Enhance Influenza Vaccination Rates," *Proceedings of the National Academy of Sciences* 108, no. 26 (2011): 10415–10420.

5 Brett Tomlinson, "Behave!," *Princeton Alumni Weekly*, October 26, 2016.

6 Kevin Hartnett, "Character's Content," *Pennsylvania Gazette Magazine*, May/June 2012, 64, http://www.upenn.edu/gazette/0512/feature4_1.html.

7 University of Pennsylvania, "Behavior Change for Good," YouTube video, 1:30, October 4, 2016, https://youtu.be/7dUUqtRQG_Y.

8 "Could Solving This One Problem Solve All the Others?," by Stephen Dubner, produced by Eliza Lambert, *Freakonomics Radio*, April 5, 2017, http://freakonomics.com/podcast/solving-one-problem-solve-others/.

9 Dan Acland and Matthew Levy, "Naivete, Project Bias, and Habit Formation in Gym Attendance," *Management Science* 61, no. 1 (2015): 146–160; Gary Charness and Uri Gneezy, "Incentives to Exercise," *Econometrica* 77, no. 3 (2009): 909–931; Heather Royer, Mark F. Stehr, and Justin R. Sydnor, "Incentives, Commitments, and Habit Formation in Exercise: Evidence from a Field Experiment with Workers at a Fortune-500 Company," *American Economic Journal: Applied Economics* 7, no. 3 (2014): 51–84. In 2017, Katy replicated the studies above, randomizing employees at a Fortune 500 company into a program that sent participants four weeks of reminders and small workout incentives. Forty weeks after the intervention ended, those who received the reminders and incentives recorded 33% more weekly gym visits than the control group (0.38 weekly workouts in the treatment group versus 0.29 weekly workouts in the control). For more see John Beshears, Katherine Milkman, Hae Nim Lee, and Rob Mislavsky, "Creating Exercise Habits Using Incentives: The Tradeoff between Flexibility and Routinization," working paper, last modified August 11, 2017.

10 Tainya C. Clarke, Tina Norris, and Jeannine S. Schiller, "Early Release of Selected Estimates Based on Data from 2016 National Health Interview Survey," National Center for Health Statistics, 2017, 43.

11 FMCG and Retail, "Healthy Aspirations: The Disconnect between Americans' Desire for a Healthy Lifestyle and Actual Behavior," Nielsen Newswire, August 4, 2014, http://www.nielsen.com/us/en/insights/news/2014/healthy-aspirations-the-disconnect-between-americans-desire-for-a-healthy-lifestyle-and-actual-behavior.html.

12 I-Min Lee, Eric J. Shiroma, Felipe Lobelo, Pekka Puska, Steven N. Blair, Peter T. Katzmarzyk, and Lancet Physical Activity Series Working Group, "Effect of Physical Inactivity on Major Non-communicable Diseases Worldwide: An Analysis of Burden of Disease and Life Expectancy," *Lancet* 380, no. 9838 (2012): 219–229.

13 Earl S. Ford, Umed A. Ajani, Janet B. Croft, Julia A. Critchley, Darwin R. Labarthe, Thomas E. Kottke, Wayne H. Giles, and Simon Capewell,

"Explaining the Decrease in U.S. Deaths from Coronary Disease, 1980–2000," *New England Journal of Medicine* 356 (2007): 2388–2398.

14 Frank Napolitano, case interview, December 4, 2017.

15 Blink Fitness, "70+ Locations," accessed October 3 2018, https://www.blinkfitness.com/locations?icmp=hdr_module_locations.

16 Interview with Ellen Roggemann.

17 "How to Launch a Behavior-Change Revolution," by Stephen Dubner, produced by Greg Rosalsky, *Freakonomics Radio*, October 25, 2017, http://freakonomics.com/podcast/launch-behavior-change-revolution/.

Chapter 14

1 Harry M. Marks, *The Progress of Experiment: Science and Therapeutic Reform in the United States, 1900–1990* (Cambridge: Cambridge University Press, 1997).

Chapter 15

1 Bruce Sacerdote, "Peer Effects with Random Assignment: Results for Dartmouth Roommates," *Quarterly Journal of Economics* 116, no. 2 (2001): 681–704.

2 Jonathan Smith, "Peers, Pressure, and Performance at the National Spelling Bee," *Journal of Human Resources* 48, no. 2 (2013): 265–285.

3 David Clingingsmith, Asim Ijaz Khwaja, and Michael Kremer, "Estimating the Impact of the Hajj: Religion and Tolerance in Islam's Global Gathering," *Quarterly Journal of Economics* 124 (2009): 1133–1170, https://doi.org/10.1162/qjec.2009.124.3.1133.

4 Julie Berry Cullen, Brian A. Jacob, and Steven Levitt, "The Effect of School Choice on Participants: Evidence from Randomized Lotteries," *Econometrica* 74, no. 5 (2006): 1191–1230. https://www.jstor.org/stable/3805923.

Index

Abdul Latif Jameel Poverty Action
  Lab (J-PAL), 42–43, 165
A/B testing, 175
Advertising, 55, 62
  eBay experiment, 94–95
  efficacy of, 92–93, 96–97
  experiment design, 97
  and Google searches, 91
  keyword, 91, 95
  platform, 92
  search, 96–97
  size of, 73
Airbnb, 77–90, 116, 128–129
  African American guests, 81–83
  design changes, 84–87
  discrimination, 79–83, 87, 184
  guest rejection, 77
  host/guest photos, 85–87
  instant booking, 86
#AirbnbWhileBlack, 84
Alcott, Hunt, 52
Alibaba, 99–104
  discounts, 99–100
  long-term effects, 103

program design, 102–103
  shopping cart experiment,
    100–101
Amazon, 73, 116, 120
Analyst Institute, 140–141
Anderson, Eric, 62
"Anomalies," 40
Anonymity, Internet, 75, 78
Asian Disease Problem, 36–38
Augustus, emperor, 154
Availability heuristic, 35
Average treatment effect, 9

Babcock, Linda, 40
Backend fees, 107, 109
Banaji, Mahzarin, 24–25
Banerjee, Abhijit, 42
Bargaining behavior, 28
Behavioral economics, 35, 39–41,
  63. See also Experimental
  economics
Behavioral experiments, 132, 135–
  143. See also Policy experiments
  diffusion of groups, 135–137

Behavioral experiments (cont.)
  economics, 28, 33, 35
  education, 145–153, 165
  field experiments, 165
  financial planning and literacy,
    154–158, 165
  and government, 61, 135
  health, 158–160, 165, 167–170
  and nudging, 52–58
  psychology, 19–20
  and theory, 185
  and voting, 138–143
Behavioral Insights Group, Harvard,
  137, 165, 175–176
Behavior Change for Good (BCFG),
  162, 164–171, 185
  exercise participation experiment,
    167–170
  lessons of, 170–171
  StepUp, 169–170
  structure, 166–167
Behavioural Insights Team (BIT),
  4–5, 41, 61, 63,
  135–137
  goals and evolution, 56–58
  tax letter experiment, 5–9, 136
Benartzi, Shlomo, 156
Berg, Gunhild, 157
Bergman, Peter, 151
Bertrand, Marianne, 82, 156
Beshears, John, 160
Bible, 9–10
Bing, 73
Blake, Tom, 94, 108
Blink Fitness, 168–169
Blocking, 13
Bohnet, Iris, 40
Booking.com, 71–73
Brain imaging, 20, 25

Brown v. Board of Education of Topeka,
  Kansas, 23–24
Bruhn, Mariam, 157

Camerer, Colin, 30, 40, 166
Cameron, David, 56
Campbell Soup Company, 61, 116
Car sales, 76–77
Castleman, Ben, 146–147, 153
Cauterization, 11
Center for Public Leadership (CPL),
  175–176
Chamberlin, Edward, 28
Chan, Eric, 151
Choi, James, 156
Choice architecture, 49–51
Cialdini, Robert, 4, 136, 142, 166
Clark, Mamie and Kenneth, 24
Classical conditioning, 19
Clingingsmith, David, 180
Clinical trials, 10–11, 13
College roommate matching,
  177–179
Confederates, 21
Consent to experimentation, 126
Consortium of Behavioral Scientists,
  139
Control groups, 8, 12
Cullen, Julie Berry, 180

Dai, Daisy, 96
Dai, Hengchen, 100
Data gathering, 66–67, 118
Dearing, Eric, 150
Debbie Downer skit, 124
Decision making, 25, 29–30, 35, 40,
  163
  choice architecture, 50–51
  correlations in, 95

dual systems model, 50–51
  and experimentation, 184–185
  managerial, 99, 103–104
  nudging, 49–51
  rationality of, 29–30, 35–36, 40
  status quo bias, 53–54
  unpredictability of, 68–69
Defined benefit plans, 154–155
Deliberate practice intervention, 153
Dependent variables, 8
Development economics, 41–43
Diet experiment, 159
Discrimination, 76–83, 87, 184
Doll studies, 24
Donaker, Geoff, 96
Dong, Lingxiu, 100
Drug delivery experiment, 160
Dual systems model, 50
Dubner, Steve, 167
Duckworth, Angela, 151–153,
  161–170, 176, 185
Duflo, Esther, 42, 155
Dweck, Carol, 152–153, 166

eBay, 65–66, 74, 92–96, 185
  ads experiment, 94–95
  and Google ads, 93
E-commerce, 75–76
Economics. *See* Experimental
  economics
Edelman, Ben, 78, 81–82
Educational outcomes, 42
Education research, 145–153, 165
  deliberate practice intervention,
    153
  financial literacy, 157–158
  grit, 151–153
  growth mindset intervention,
    152–153

and social norms, 151
  student attendance interventions,
    148–151
  summer melt experiment, 146–147
  traits/skill dichotomy, 152
  unintended consequences,
    149–150
Emojis, 52
Eskreis-Winkler, Lauren, 153
Essay Concerning Human Understanding,
  An, 17–18
Estrogen, 13–14
Ethics of experimentation, 125–127,
  173–176
Evaluation of design changes, 89–90,
  184
Exercise participation experiment,
  167–170
Expected utility theory, 36–37
Expedia, 77
Experimental economics, 26–34.
  See also Experimentation; Policy
  experiments
  behavioral experiments, 28, 33,
    35
  field experiments, 41–43
  game theory, 28, 33
  goals of, 31
  laboratory experiments, 28–29
  market mechanisms, 29–30
  and psychology, 34–36, 40
  rationality of decision making,
    29–30, 35–36, 40
  rules of, 29
Experimental psychology, 17–26. *See*
  also Experimentation
  behaviorism, 19–20
  deception, 29
  and economics, 34–36, 40

Experimental psychology (cont.)
  Implicit Associations Test (IAT),
    24–25
  institutional review boards (IRB),
    23
  laboratories, 18
  obedience-to-authority
    experiments, 20–23
  rationality, 29
  social psychology, 20–23
*Experimental Psychology: A Manual of
  Laboratory Practice*, 18
Experimentation. *See also*
    Experimental economics;
    Experimental psychology
  barriers to, 64–69
  benefits of, 73–74, 88–90, 131–132,
    182
  conflicting incentives, 112
  and consent, 126
  data gathering, 66–68, 118
  and decision making, 184–185
  ethics of, 125–127, 173–176
  features of, 182
  growth of, 16
  long-term/short-term outcomes,
    103, 110–112, 131, 160, 170
  and managerial decisions, 99
  market-level, 116–119
  online platforms, 69
  as series of experiments, 104,
    131
  spillover effects, 115–116
  transparency, 89, 128–130, 132,
    186
  unintended consequences, 52,
    149–150
  uses of, 182–183
Experiment aversion, 175, 186–187

Facebook, 121–132
  algorithm, 121
  and election of 2016, 122
  ethics of experimentation,
    125–127
  News Feed, 121–123
  positive/negative posts
    experiments, 123–124
  transparency, 128–130
  user reaction, 124–125
Fact finding, 90, 185
Fee strategy experiment, 108–109
Feller, Avi, 148–149
Feminine Forever, 13
Field experiments, 41–43, 65
Financial planning, 154–158, 165
  financial literacy experiments,
    157
  payday lending experiment,
    156–157
  retirement saving experiments,
    155–156
Fisher, Ronald, 13
Fouraker, Lawrence E., 28
401k plans, 52
Fox, Craig, 139–140
Frameworks, 185
Framing, 38
Freud, Sigmund, 19
Fryer, Roland, 38

Game theory, 28, 33
Gap, The, 92
Generalizability, 34
Gerber, Alan, 138–140
Gilchrist, Duncan, 115, 117–120
Glennerster, Rachel, 42
Goldstein, Dan, 45
Gollwitzer, Peter, 142

Google, 63, 70–71
  and eBay ads, 93–94
  search algorithm, 91–92
Gosnell, Harold, 138
Government
  and behavioral experiments, 61,
    135
  as choice architect, 49
  policy experiments, 56–58
Grant, Adam, 166
Green, Donald, 138–139
Greenwald, Tony, 24
Grit, 151–153
Growth mindset intervention,
  152–153
Guillory, Jamie, 123

Hajj pilgrimage, 180
Hall, G. Stanley, 18
Hallsworth, Michael, 4, 6
Halperin, Basil, 119
Halpern, David, 4, 56, 176
Hancock, Jeffrey, 123
Harrison, Glenn, 41
Harvard Behavioral Insights Group,
  137, 165
Hauser, Oliver, 177
Health experiments, 165
  diet, 159
  drug delivery, 160
  exercise participation, 167–170
  insurance, 27
  medication, 158–159
  temptation bundling, 159
  vaccination rates, 159
Heart disease, 15
Heckman, Jim, 166
Her Majesty's Revenue and Customs
  (HMRC), 3–6

Ho, Benjamin, 119
Holder, Eric, 84
Hormone replacement therapy
  (HRT), 13–15

Ideas42, 137
Implementation intentions,
  141–142
Implicit Associations Test (IAT),
  24–25
Implicit bias, 25
Incidental experiments, 177–180
Independent variables, 8
Innovation, 118
Institutional review boards, 23
Insurance experiment, 27
International Finance Corporation,
  137
Internet
  anonymity, 75, 78
  and discrimination, 76–83, 87
Interventions, efficacy of, 157
"I Paid $2,500 for a 'Hamilton'
  Ticket," 105
Issenberg, Sasha, 140–141

Jacob, Brian, 180
James, William, 18
Johnson, Eric, 45
J-PAL. See Abdul Latif Jameel Poverty
  Action Lab
"Judgment under Uncertainty:
  Heuristics and Biases," 35

Kahneman, Daniel, 28, 34–39, 41,
  50, 136, 175
Kennedy, Reed, 79–82
Kenyan textbook problem, 42
Kerry, John, 142

Kessler, Judd, 47–48
Keyword advertising, 91, 95
Khwaja, Asim, 180
Kim, Hyunjin, 96
Kohavi, Ron, 73
Kramer, Adam, 123
Kremer, Michael, 42, 180

Laboratory experiments, 28–29,
    54–55
Laibson, David, 40
Leadership, 176, 181
Leamer, Edward, 26
Lee, Monica, 150
Letters, experimental, 5–6, 136
Levitt, Steven, 38, 54, 180
Lewin, Kurt, 20
Lewis, Michael, 34
Lind, James, 11
List, John, 36, 38, 41, 54, 119
Locke, John, 17
Loewenstein, George, 30, 32, 40
Longevity, 16
Long-term/short-term outcomes of
    experimentation, 103, 110–112,
    131, 160, 170
Loss aversion, 159
Lotteries, 179–180
Lusardi, Annamaria, 155

Madrian, Brigitte, 155
Magnetic resonance, 20, 25
Magnitude of an effect, 54–55
Managerial decisions, 99, 103–104
Mankiw, N. Gregory, 105
Manson, JoAnn, 15
Market creation, 113
Market efficiency, 106
Market-level experiments, 116–119
Market mechanisms, 29–30

Marks, Harry, 175
Massachusetts organ donation
    experiment, 47–48
Mathematica Policy Research, 27
Mechanism experiments, 184–185
Medical research, 13–16
Medical Research Council (MRC), 13
Medication compliance experiment,
    158–159
Mental philosophy, 17
Microsoft, 73–74
Milgram, Stanley, 20–22
Milkman, Katherine, 139, 159,
    161–170, 176, 185
Morse, Adair, 156
Morton, Fiona Scott, 76
Moshary, Sarah, 108
Muir, Ian, 119
Mullainathan, Sendhil, 40, 42, 82,
    166
Murnighan, Keith, 32–34
Murphy, Laura, 84

Napolitano, Frank, 168
National Spelling Bee, 179
Natural field experiments, 41
Nazism, 20–21
Nesta, 58
Newhouse, Joe, 27
New Jersey Income Maintenance
    Experiment, 27
New Yorker cartoons, 75–76, 78–79
Nosko, Chris, 94
Nudge4 Solutions Lab, 147
*Nudge: Improving Decisions about
    Health, Wealth, and Happiness*, 40,
    146
Nudging, 49–58
    and behavioral experiments, 52–55
    and decision making, 49–51

lab and field contexts, 54–55
nudge unit, 56–58
Nurses' Health Study, 14

Obama, Michelle, 147
Obedience-to-authority
    experiments, 20–23
Oligopolies, 28
Olken, Benjamin, 43
100&Change, 161
Online platforms, 69, 77
Online shopping, 75–76
Operant conditioning, 19
Opt-in/opt-out policies, 45–47, 49
Organ donations, 45–49
Organic links, 91, 94
Ostrovsky, Michael, 73
Overconfidence, 69

Page, Lindsay, 146–147, 153
Paktor, 72
Paré, Ambroise, 11
Pasteur, Louis, 12
Pavlov, Ivan, 19
Pavlovian conditioning, 19
Payday lending experiment,
    156–157
Perfect competition, theory of,
    28
Peysakovich, Alex, 122
Phrenology, 18
Physiological measures, 20, 25
Policy experiments, 27–28,
    40–41, 61. See also Behavioral
    experiments
  active choice, 46–48
  default settings, 48, 50, 52
  design choices, 52
  government, 56–58
  nudging, 49–58

opt-in/opt-out policies, 45–47,
    49–50
organ donation, 47–48
unintended consequences, 52
Pope, Devin, 38
Poverty reduction, 42–43
Present bias, 155, 158
Presidential election of 2016, 122
Profitability, 174
"Prospect Theory: An Analysis of
    Decisions under Risk," 35
Psychology. See Experimental
    psychology
Putin, Vladimir, 122

Rabin, Matthew, 40
Racial segregation, 24
Racism, 24–25, 76, 83
RAND Corporation, 27
Random assignment, 13–15,
    178–179
Randomization, 65–66
Randomized control clinical trials,
    13, 154
Rao, Justin, 95
Rational behavior, 29–30, 35–36, 40
Rental markets, 78
Replication, 13
Representativeness heuristic, 35
Retail catalogs, 62
Retirement planning, 154–156
Retirement saving experiments,
    155–156
Rideshare companies, 113, 183
Risk-averse/risk-seeking behavior,
    37–38
Robinson, Carly, 150
Rogers, Todd, 139–142, 145,
    147–149, 151, 153, 159, 163, 185
Roggemann, Ellen, 169

Roommate matching, 177–179
Ross, Heather, 27
Rossignol, Hippolyte, 12
Roth, Al, 31–34, 47–48, 54, 104
Roussos, Chris, 168

Sacerdote, Bruce, 178–179
Sadoff, Sally, 38
Saez, Emmanuel, 155
Sample size, 64–65
Sauermann, Heinz, 28
"Save More Tomorrow" plan, 156
Scaling, 135
Schwarz, Michael, 73
Scurvy, 11–12
Search advertising, 96–97
Search algorithm, Google, 91–92
Selection bias, 14, 93
Selten, Reinhard, 28
Service, Owain, 4, 56
Shea, Dennis, 155
Shopping cart experiment, 100–101
Short-term/long-term outcomes of
    experimentation, 103, 110–112,
    131, 160, 170
Siegel, Sidney, 28
Silva-Risso, Jorge, 76
Simester, Duncan, 62
Simon, Herbert, 29
Simonov, Andrey, 95
Skinner, B. F., 19
Small business advertising, 96–97
Smith, Jonathan, 179
Smith, Vernon, 28–32
Social and Behavioral Science
    Initiative, 58
Social comparisons, 149, 151
Social norms, 151
Social psychology, 20–23

Spillover effects, 115–116
Stanovich, Keith, 50
Statistical discrimination, 83
Status quo bias, 53–54
Stephens-Davidowitz, Seth, 123
Stereotypes, 24–25, 83
Streptomycin, 13
StubHub, 73, 105–112
    ethics of ticket resale, 105–106
    fees, 107–109
    fee strategy experiment, 108–109
    long-term outcomes, 110–112
Student attendance interventions,
    148–151
Summer melt experiment, 146–147
Summer Melt: Supporting Low-Income
    Students through the Transition to
    College, 147
Sunstein, Cass, 40, 49, 52
Svirsky, Dan, 81–82
Sweeney, Kane, 108

Tadelis, Steve, 92–94, 108
Tax letter trials, 5–9, 136
Tech companies, 62–64, 183
    economics experimentation,
        119–120
    lessons of experimentation,
        130–131
    and randomization, 65–66
    returns on experimentation, 73–74
    transparency, 129–130, 132
Temptation bundling, 159
Testing theories, 88, 184–185
Thaler, Richard, 39–41, 49, 52, 136,
    156, 166, 176
Thinking, Fast and Slow, 34, 50
Titchener, Edward Bradford, 18
Tradeoffs, 89

Transparency, 89, 128–130, 132, 186
Treatment groups, 8
Trump, Donald, 122
Tversky, Amos, 34–38, 41, 136, 175
24 Hour Fitness, 168–169

uAspire, 146
Uber, 65, 113–120, 183
  Express Pool experiment, 117–118,
    184
  innovation, 118
  options, 114
  spillover effects, 115–116
  tipping experiments, 119
Uber Express Pool, 114–115,
  117–118
Uncertainty, 186
Undoing Project, The, 4
Unequal treatment, 173
Unintended consequences, 52,
  149–150
United States
  election of 2016, 122
  medical research, 15–16
  organ donation, 46–47
  student absenteeism, 148
  voter turnout, 138
Unpredictability, 68–69

Vaccination, 12
Vacuum experiment, 67–68
Variables, dependent/independent,
  8
Varian, Hal, 71, 176
Vermeer, Lukas, 72
Victory Lab, The, 140–141
Volpp, Kevin, 158–159
Voter turnout, 138, 143
Voting, 138–143

Watson, John, 19
Wealthfront, 120
West, Richard, 50
Wilson, Robert, 13–14
Women's Health Initiative, 15
Wundt, Wilhelm, 18

Yahoo, 73
Yeager, David, 153
Yelp ads, 96–97, 116

Zettelmeyer, Florian, 76
Zhang, Dennis, 100
Zia, Bilal, 157
Zimbardo, Philip, 20, 22–23
Zlatev, Julian, 48